Talk Thru Bible Personalities

DEDICATION

Dedicated to Matthew Libby, David Wilkinson
and Jennifer Wilkinson . . . our children.

May the enduring lessons of these men and
women burn in your hearts, light
your way, and kindle an unquenchable longing
to walk with the living God.

"Everything that was written in the past was
written to teach us, so that through
endurance and the encouragement of
the Scriptures we might have hope."
(Romans 15:4 NIV.)

Published by Walk Thru the Bible Ministries, Inc. Printed in the United States of
America. First printing, September 1983.

Library of Congress Catalog Card Number 83-50663
ISBN 0-9612142-0-1

Unless otherwise indicated, Scripture quotations are from the New International Version of the Bible.

INTRODUCTION

One of the most remarkable teaching methods God uses with His children *today* is that of drawing upon lessons He has taught other members of the household of faith in the *past.*

The Scriptures are full of historical illustrations with contemporary applications. "These things happened to them as examples and were written down as warnings for us . . ." (1 Cor. 10:11a NIV).

The experiences of life—both good and bad—become living object lessons to those who will but take the time to notice and profit. All too often, however, the pace of life robs us of those reflective moments, and the object lessons remain unlearned. We neither profit from—nor pass on to others—God's precious truth, and the teaching cycle breaks down.

Talk Thru Bible Personalities is our attempt to pass on to you some of the key life-changing principles we've observed in the lives of twelve personalities from the pages of the Bible. May these men and women, though dead, remain as living teachers to us all each time we meet them in God's Word.

Bruce H. Wilkinson   Larry Libby
Founder and President   Multnomah Press
Walk Thru the Bible Ministries   Portland, Oregon
Atlanta, Georgia

Contents

Jacob

Jacob

It's doubtful that Jacob ever saw himself as a saint. Much less an important historical figure, a "Bible Personality" or the founder of a great nation. Jacob was much too busy being Jacob. A man with a long shopping list of hopes and fears and secret dreams. A human being just like you.

Jacob was a man who fervently believed in God—earnestly wanted to be a good husband and father—but a man who ran into frustration after frustration, disappointment after disappointment.

For most of his life, Jacob found himself riding a spiritual roller coaster. Climbing to peaks of spiritual awareness, then plunging into valleys of empty striving. Up and down, round and round. Over and over. That's one big reason why Jacob's life is in the Book. Because God wants something better for you. Paul said it like this: "Everything that was written in the past was written to teach us, so that through endurance and the encouragement of the Scriptures we might have hope" (Rom. 15:4 NIV).

God wants to encourage you . . . to draw on His inexhaustible resources, to become His constant companion, to find the fountain of your strength and joy in Him.

Everyone has ups and downs, but through the life of this man you can learn how to take the principles God teaches you on those rare spiritual mountaintops and put them to work in the day-by-day valleys of your life.

Unless otherwise indicated, Scripture quotations in this chapter are from the New American Standard Bible.

Striving for Blessing
(Genesis 25-28)

*J*ust as the blessing and promise of God passed from Abraham to Isaac, they must also pass from Isaac to his son. But Isaac's wife, Rebekah, has twin sons: Esau and Jacob. Because Esau emerges from the womb first, the birthright and blessing rightfully belong to him.

Jacob, however, manages to obtain the birthright from his careless brother by a trade and later conspires with his mother to steal the fatherly blessing as well.

Having blessed Jacob, Isaac sends him to Paddan-aram (Haran) to find a wife from among the daughters of Laban, Abraham's kinsman and brother of Rebekah. While on his journey, Jacob stops to sleep and has a vision. In it he sees the Lord standing at the top of a ladder stretching into heaven. In this dramatic way, the Lord speaks to Jacob and reaffirms the covenant made with Abraham and Issac. God's specific promise to Jacob is that through his descendants God will bless all nations.

Focus	Striving for Blessing (Genesis 25-28)				
Divisions	Born as the younger of twins	"Buys" Esau's birthright	Steals Esau's blessing	Flees Esau's wrath	Dreams at Bethel; bargain with God
Topics	Struggles With Family				
	Jacob's Call				
	Bethel/"God's House"				
Place	Canaan				
Approx. Dates (Age)	2005–1928 B.C. (Birth–77 yrs.)				

Striving for Prosperity
(Genesis 29-31)

*H*onoring the desires of Isaac, Jacob arrives in Haran to find a wife. Here he finds Rachel, daughter of Laban, and falls in love with her. Jacob pledges to serve Laban for seven years for the right to marry Rachel. After the seven years, however, Laban tricks Jacob by giving him Leah, his older daughter, on the wedding night. Because of his great desire for Rachel, Jacob agrees to work another seven years in order to marry Rachel as well. In a bitter rivalry to produce heirs for Jacob, the two sisters each give Jacob their maids to be his concubines. From these four women, twelve sons are born to Jacob.

Following the birth of Joseph, Jacob decides to leave Laban's land and return to the land of his father. After major strife over the ownership of property, a wealthy Jacob and his large family depart from Paddan-aram.

Striving for Godliness
(Genesis 32-50)

*A*fter finally parting company with his contentious father-in-law, Jacob immediately encounters new trouble. He learns that Esau, his rightfully bitter twin brother, is coming to meet him with 400 men. Jacob is gripped with fear, supposing that Esau was coming to seek revenge.

On the night before Esau is to arrive, Jacob encounters the Angel of the Lord and wrestles with Him until daybreak. As a result of that night-long wrestling match, God changes Jacob's name to Israel, meaning "prince with God."

Upon reaching Canaan, Jacob first settles near Shechem. After strife with the Shechemites, however, he answers God's summons and returns to Bethel.

When his son, Joseph, becomes a high official in the land of Egypt, Jacob and all his family move into that country to escape the ravages of famine in Canaan. Jacob dies in Egypt, but his sons carry him back to Hebron, in Canaan, where he is buried.

Striving for Prosperity (Genesis 29–31)			Striving for Godliness (Genesis 32–50)					
Married Leah and Rachel	Raises 11 children; becomes prosperous	Strives with Laban, flees to Canaan	Wrestles with God	Encounters Esau	Finds trouble near Shechem	Returns to Bethel; spiritual renewal	Reunited with Joseph, sojourns in Egypt	Dies in Egypt; buried in Haran
Struggles With In-Laws			Struggles With God					
Jacob's Marriage			Jacob's Return					
Manahaim/"God's Host"			Peniel/"God's Face"					
Haran			Canaan/Egypt					
1928–1908 B.C. (77–97 yrs.)			1908–1858 B.C. (97–147 yrs.)					

A Mountain Called Bethel

(Read: Genesis 27-28)

Wittingly or unwittingly, Jacob becomes a classic example of a man who lives up to his own bad name. The name "Jacob" literally means *supplanter* or *deceiver*. Turning his back on God's wisdom and power, Jacob turns again and again to his own cunning and scheming to face the challenges of life.

Only three verses into Jacob's biography, the account reveals the first clear example of "Deceiver" living out the meaning of his name (Gen. 25:29-34). Even though his brother Esau, the first-born, is entitled to receive the birthright from Isaac, Jacob will employ any strategy to obtain it for himself.

The stew-for-birthright deal seems good enough to a hungry Esau at the time his shrewd brother suggests the arrangement. But the warm satisfaction of a good-tasting meal fades all too quickly as the realization of a great loss erupts in brother Esau's emotions. Jacob has really only one choice: to flee for his life. It is on his way to safety at his Uncle Laban's distant sheep ranch that Isaac's youngest son experiences a dramatic encounter with the God of heaven and earth.

Until this time, everything that has been revealed about Jacob has reference to his own self-effort, his own self-interest and his own self-preservation. Now, however, God reaches down and tries to impress upon Jacob that there is more to life than that which is earthly, human and self-centered. God wants to knock the blinders off Jacob's eyes and free him from a restrictive case of tunnel vision. And God's therapy is unusual—He sends Jacob a dream. With a stone for a pillow, the travel-weary Jacob falls asleep. Before he awakens, he will experience one of those unfor-gettable "nights of the soul" where he meets God as never before.

In Jacob's dream, a great ladder spans the distance between earth and heaven. While angels climb up and down the ladder, God Himself stands above it, talking to His servant: "I am the Lord, the God of your father Abraham and the God of Isaac; the land on which you lie, I will give it to you and to your descen-dants . . . . And behold, I am with you, and will keep you wherever you go" (Gen. 28:13,15).

Through the ladder, God is showing Jacob that there is no gulf between heaven and earth for the one who knows Him. The ladder and the angels symbolize free access from the believer on earth to the Lord in heaven. Pointed message to Jacob: There is no need to tackle the problems of life by anxiously trying to figure out all the angles. Open to every believer is the very real potential of living out this earthly existence on the basis of heavenly wisdom and fellowship. The ladder is there; God is there. But the ladder must be used; God must be approached.

Jacob awakes, absolutely awestruck. He has encountered God . . . and he knows it. "Surely the Lord is in this place," he whispers. "How awesome is this place! This is none other than the house of God, and this is the gate of heaven" (Gen. 28:16,17). Jacob is overwhelmed. He builds an altar on the site of this "spiritual mountain peak" and names the place *Bethel* ("House of God"). Before leaving, Jacob vows that if God will protect him and meet his needs "then the Lord will be my God" (Gen. 28:21). Jacob is a changed man! Or so it seems . . . .

Do you remember your last spiritual mountaintop? Perhaps it was a weekend retreat and somehow it seemed as though the speaker had studied your life history before preparing his message. His words hit you exactly where you were, and you were moved. In fact, you even promised God you would . . . . Or maybe it was that Bible study last month. So rich! It warmed your heart to the core and you told God you would . . . . Then again it might have been that special church service last week or last month or last year. The pastor aimed words which the Spirit of God turned into arrows that pierced your shell and made you think and weep and promise to . . . .

Jacob's encounter with God at Bethel surely had that kind of profound impact on his life, too. Unfortunately, the events that follow reveal that this towering mountaintop experience has little impact on Jacob's daily lifestyle.

The Valley Of Laban

(Read: Genesis 29-31)

Nothing is more ironic than when the cheater is cheated, the thief is robbed, or the murderer is murdered. As Jacob settles in at his Uncle Laban's home, the schemer finds himself temporarily out-schemed. Jacob falls in love with Laban's youngest daughter, Rachel, and agrees with Laban to put in seven years of labor to get Rachel as his wife. But then Laban pulls a "Jacob." Instead of giving Rachel to Jacob for a wife, he makes a quick switch at the last moment and substitutes his older daughter, Leah. In order for Jacob to actually get Rachel, Laban requires another seven years of ranch work. Jacob is furious, but so helplessly in love with the young woman that he agrees to the added years on his uncle's payroll (Gen. 29:15-30).

A few more years go by and Jacob decides to leave Laban's "hospitality." But Laban is not willing to lose such a hard-working ranch hand. So he makes another deal. Before the ink is dry on the contract, however, Laban takes cunning steps to cut the heart out of Jacob's benefits in the deal. First, he allows Jacob to lay down the conditions of the transaction. Jacob is to go through the flocks of sheep and goats and take for himself all those that are spotted and speckled. These are to become the possession of Jacob, and to this Laban agrees. But as soon as his son-in-law turns his back, Laban rounds up all the spotted animals and herds them a three-day journey from his ranch.

Not willing to be outdone in a contest of wits, Jacob counterattacks with a strategy that effectively out-maneuvers his uncle's maneuvers (Gen. 30:37-31:55). Once again, Jacob's carefully-crafted deceptions win the day. And once again, Jacob is forced to flee . . . .

Obviously, Jacob is riding the roller coaster. The awesome experience with God at Bethel has become simply that—an awesome experience. Instead of plugging into God's availability and power for everyday living, Jacob has Bethel neatly shelved under the label: "Exciting Spiritual Experiences of the Past." That which was to prepare him for his encounter with Laban in the "valley" has become little more than an interesting memory.

But wasn't Laban's trickery shameful? Didn't he richly deserve everything his nephew dished out to him? Wasn't Jacob's revenge only natural? Perhaps . . . *but not in the light of Bethel.* Jacob had seen the ladder. Jacob had witnessed the mighty, ministering angels and had reclined at the very gate of heaven. Jacob had heard the voice of God—had become aware of the heavenly means to deal with earthly issues. He knew the better way! And yet he stooped to his old methods, dusted off his old tricks. His old lifestyle of wiles and wit fit like a comfortable slipper—this business of resting in God seemed so frightening. So instead of placing his distressing in-law problems into the willing hands of his God, Jacob insisted on taking matters into his own hands.

Looking back on Jacob's failures in this "down" time of his life, you might wonder: "What did he do that was so terrible?" Jacob was simply an ambitious young man who wanted to get ahead. Nothing wrong with that, is there? Today he might be called a "wheeler-dealer," an "entrepreneur," or "bullish." A bright young junior-executive type who knew how to take advantage of every situation. According to the world's standards, Jacob had simply acted in his own best interests.

But Jacob had another standard—the standard of his God. The standard of the One who had personally revealed Himself to Jacob, the One who had said, "I am with you and will keep you wherever you go." Much had been given to Jacob; much was required. God expected something more: He expected calm trust instead of anxious conniving; dependence on spiritual resources rather than desperate scrambling and deceitful scheming. God wanted so much for the heavenly ladder to become Jacob's *daily resource*, rather than his *occasional recourse*. He wanted Bethel to be a vital part of Jacob's moment-by-moment experience, rather than some misty spiritual mountaintop of the past.

A Mountain Called Peniel

(Read: Genesis 32:1-33:17)

With his back to the deception and discouragement of his stay with Uncle Laban, Jacob turns his face toward the south—the land of his birth. But not only is he returning to the land of his birth, he is also returning to the land of his *brother*. Twenty-year-old fears surge across his emotions. Esau's last comment had been something less than comforting. Jacob's mother, Rebekah, had told him: "Behold your brother Esau is consoling himself concerning you, by planning to kill you" (Gen. 27:42).

God knew Jacob would panic. But rather than abandoning His servant for being so faithless and fearful, God takes incredible measures to encourage and reassure him. As the anxious man journeys, God meets him in a mysterious way. "Now as Jacob went on his way, the angels of God met him. And Jacob said when he saw them, 'This is God's camp.' So he named that place Mahanaim" (Gen. 32:1,2).

Jacob is awed—but again fails to understand the message. Instead, he throws himself into a desperate planning session. Perhaps flattery will appease his brother! Jacob sends servants ahead and lays it on thick: "My *lord* Esau" . . . "your *servant* Jacob . . . ." But then the servants return with the bone-chilling message: "We came to your brother Esau, and furthermore he is coming to meet you, *and four hundred men are with him*" (Gen. 32:6, italics added).

Now Jacob's panic explodes into flames. But instead of turning to God, he throws his mental computer into overdrive. Strategy after desperate strategy tumbles in his mind. Maybe bribery will save the day! Jacob sends his servants ahead to meet Esau with generous gifts. Obviously expecting the worst, he divides his family and servants into two companies.

"Then Jacob was left alone, and a man wrestled with him until daybreak" (Gen. 32:24). This mysterious night wrestler is none other than God Himself, in the form of a man. Up to this point, Jacob's all-consuming thought has been the coming confrontation with his brother. Now, he finds himself in a face-to-face encounter with his God.

So tenacious is Jacob's opposition that the Lord is forced to wound him. "And when he saw that he had not prevailed against him, he touched the socket of his thigh; so the socket of Jacob's thigh was dislocated while he wrestled" (Gen. 32:25).

Who wins this mysterious wrestling bout? Jacob is hurt, but refuses to release his divine opponent. "I will not let you go unless you bless me" (Gen. 32:26). The Lord has been pursuing Jacob for years. Now, wounded, alone and frightened—at the most critical moment of his life—Jacob clings to God with all of his strength. Even as the night begins to pale in the east, the light of understanding is finally penetrating Jacob's heart. Life is not simply a matter of doing your best, trying your hardest, being the most clever—life for the believer means walking in the presence and power of God. That was God's message to Jacob at Bethel, but Jacob didn't see it. That was God's message at Mahanaim, but Jacob didn't understand.

But now Jacob sees—now he grasps the message. Centuries later, the prophet Hosea will offer this divine commentary: "In the womb he (Jacob) took his brother by the heel, and in his maturity he contended with God. Yes, he wrestled with the angel and prevailed; he wept and sought His favor. He found Him at Bethel" (Hos. 12:3,4).

"What is your name?" the Wrestler asks Jacob.

"Jacob," he replies.

"Your name shall no longer be Jacob, but Israel; for you have striven with God and with men *and have prevailed*" (Gen. 32:27,28, italics added).

Who won the wrestling match? Jacob won! But only after he had been wounded. Only after he had learned the painful lesson of dependence. And he could never, never forget that lesson. Because Jacob walked away from Peniel ("I have seen God face to face" [Gen. 32:30]) with a limp.

Of all God's many gifts to the patriarch—on the mountains and in the valleys—the limp was perhaps the most precious gift of all.

Lasting Lessons from Jacob

Two major lessons emerge from the account of this unusual man, Jacob.

First of all, God shows through the life of Jacob the bankruptcy of manipulating people to get your own way. Jacob had manipulation down to a science, and would undoubtedly have made a classic self-seeking city mayor. He had that backroom-politician's ability to successfully use people in order to achieve his own ends. With Jacob in city hall, the political machine would be fine-tuned to perfection. Jacob would be at his best ramrodding proposals through city council, lobbying key state legislators, or leaking selective bits of confidential information to an unwary press in order to discredit an opponent. He knew how to get things done—he knew how to get what he wanted.

But it wasn't God's way. Jacob didn't have to lie and cheat and scheme to get the birthright from his older brother. It had been promised to him before he was born. God could have easily accomplished that . . . if Jacob would have given him the opportunity. Jacob didn't have to resort to deceiving his old, blind father in order to obtain a blessing. God was capable of overcoming Isaac's favoritism . . . if Jacob would have given the Lord a chance. Jacob didn't have to wear out his brain trying to outwit Laban, he didn't have to conjure up a plan to appease his brother—he didn't have to do any of these things. God had told Jacob very clearly that He would be with him, protect him and bless him.

But Jacob refused God's way; refused God's timing. In so doing, *he refused God's best.*

Could it be that you have been short-circuiting God's best for your life through impatience and lack of trust? Do you find it easier to scheme and manipulate rather than to wait on the Lord and rest in Him? In the short run, using people may appear to get quick results. But God sees the whole picture. He knows where that winding road leads. And because of His love, He longs for you to find the better way.

The second major lesson stands out like a long shadow cast by the mountain experience at Peniel. Sometimes, when a child of God will not respond to His gentle voice but stubbornly persists in a self-destructive, fruitless way, God is forced to use drastic measures to get that person's attention. Sometimes, God has to wound you in order to help you. See this in the life of Jacob from a slightly different perspective:

Like a drowning man, Jacob thrashes and splashes, refusing the Lifeguard's assistance. "I'm here!" says the Lifeguard. "I can help you. I can teach you how to swim so that you won't have to struggle. Just *relax*—let Me slip My arm around you. Quit fighting Me!" But still Jacob kicks and claws at the water, vainly trying to battle his way along, not realizing that all of his strenuous efforts are totally self-defeating. Once again the Lifeguard tries reassuring words, and once again the straining man cannot—will not hear. Seeing that Jacob is about to go under and left with no other option, the Lifeguard strikes the laboring swimmer—wounding him. Weakened and dazed, Jacob can now only cling to his Rescuer. And in his clinging—he is saved.

If we compel Him to do so, God may use stern, external measures to teach us the crucially important principle of dependence. Disappointment, setbacks, loss and trying situations are all tools in the Master Surgeon's loving hands; He must cut, so that He might heal.

Have you heard the gentle voice of His Spirit recently—the clear witness of His Word—urging you to close the gap and walk by His side? Respond to His call—respond to His Word—immediately. Don't wait until the pressure of circumstances forces you to your knees . . . fall willingly, wholeheartedly, before Him . . . right now.

And if God has given you a limp, like Jacob, don't despise it. Limping through the valleys of life with God at your side is better than any mountain.

Work It Through

1. Spiritual mountaintop experiences are often associated with special *places*—a weekend retreat, a trip to the mountains, etc. In these unique settings, you are sometimes able to get a new perspective—to see your life from a fresh point of view. Can you think of three possible ways to find that same sort of perspective in the midst of your busy daily life?

_____

_____

2. What are two possible causes (and two corresponding cures) for a "spiritual roller coaster" lifestyle? To what extent should you expect emotional and spiritual ups and downs when you walk with the Lord?

_____

_____

3. Think back to the last time you felt "used" by someone else. Was it an intentional action by that person, or might it have been simply thoughtlessness? What are three practical ways you can guard against carelessly using other people to promote your own interests?

_____

_____

4. Why do you think the Angel of the Lord had to wound Jacob? Try to identify two "wounds" God has used to accomplish a similar goal in your life.

_____

_____

5. Who do you think *really* won the wrestling match at Peniel, and why?

_____

_____

NOTES

Moses

Can you remember the last time you caught a glimpse of God? Was it this morning? Last week? Two years ago?

Most likely it didn't come through a flash of lightning or a startling vision. More likely you were at the kitchen table with a cup of coffee in your hand. Or out on the back porch in a lawn chair. Or on your knees in the quiet of your bedroom. You might have been reading the Bible, meditating on some portion of Scripture or praying. Then again, you might have been in the middle of something as mundane as walking the dog, feeding the baby or driving to work, when suddenly—unexpectedly—you caught a glimpse of God. You saw Him in a new way, caught a fresh insight into His love . . . His greatness . . . His holiness. And what you saw touched your heart and made a difference in your life.

Did you know that God cherishes those moments as much as you do? He delights to be found by his seeking children. He loves to reveal Himself to those who are earnestly longing to know Him.

The life of Moses is the story of a man who enjoyed an extraordinary relationship with God. Scripture says of him that "the Lord would speak to Moses face to face, as a man speaks with his friend" (Exod. 33:11). As you read about three of Moses' encounters with God, ask God to reveal Himself to you in a fresh and vital way at the same time. Remember, Moses' God is *your* God, too. The same God who walked and talked with Old Testament men and women centuries ago, wants to walk and talk with you . . . today.

The Prince of Egypt
(Exodus 2:1-15)

*B*orn in Egypt to a Hebrew mother and father, the infant Moses was immediately in danger of being put to death by a decree of Pharaoh, who insisted that all male Hebrew babies must die. Instead of being killed, however, Moses is hidden by his godly parents. At the age of three months, he is adopted—in God's providence —by the daughter of Pharaoh and raised as her own son.

The princess unwittingly hires Moses' real mother to be the baby's nurse and it is at her knee that he learns of his true people and the one true God.

As Moses grows into manhood, he is educated in all the wisdom of Egypt— trained as a prince in the midst of the highest civilization of the times. At the age of 40, however, Moses makes the critical decision to forsake his adopted heritage and ally himself with God's enslaved people. In a fit of indignation, he kills a cruel Egyptian taskmaster and is forced to flee for his life into the desert regions of Midian.

Focus	The Prince of Egypt (Exodus 2:1–15)			
Divisions	Adopted by Pharaoh's daughter	Studies Egyptian knowledge	Slays Egyptian taskmaster	Flees to Midian
Topics	Scholar			
	40 Years of Luxury			
	Pride			
Place	Egypt			
Approx. Dates (Age)	1525–1485 B.C. (Birth–40 yrs.)			

The Shepherd of Midian
(Exodus 2:16-4:31)

*A*t a well in the desert, Moses performs a chivalrous act of kindness for the daughters of a Midianite sheep rancher named Jethro. Eventually Moses marries one of Jethro's daughters and agrees to live as an alien in Midian and tend his father-in-law's flocks.

For a period of 40 years, Moses lives the life of a simple shepherd. Content with his subordinate position, the former Egyptian prince spends countless hours of reflection and meditation as he leads his flocks through the desolate hills and valleys.

On one such excursion, Moses encounters a burning bush near the mountain called Horeb. As he draws near to the bush, God speaks to him from the flames and commissions him to lead the Israelites out of Egyptian bondage into the land promised to their fathers. Fearful and reluctant, Moses raises four different objections, each of which is answered by God.

The Shepherd of Israel
(Exodus 5–Deuteronomy 34)

*W*hen Pharaoh resists God's word through Moses that Israel must go free, Moses calls forth ten devastating plagues to fall on the land and people of Egypt. Finally, after God's angel kills all of Egypt's firstborn in one single night, Pharaoh commands Israel to leave. Moses leads the people through the divinely opened Red Sea.

Although the people grumble against their divinely appointed leader, God provides for their needs and leads them by His own presence. Moses receives the law from God's own hand on Mt. Sinai, disciplines the people when they rebel, and leads them to the very borders of the promised land. When the Israelites refuse to enter into the land, God condemns them to wander their lives away in the wilderness.

Moses, too, dies in the wilderness because of an act of disobedience. But before he dies, the aged leader gives God's law to a new generation of Israelites who will enter and possess the land.

The Shepherd of Midian (Exodus 2:16–4:31)				The Shepherd of Israel (Exodus 5–Deuteronomy 34)				
Marries into Jethro's family	Watches Jethro's flocks	Encountered God at burning bush	Departs for Egypt	Leads Exodus from Egypt	Receives the Law at Sinai	Constructs Tabernacle	Leads in the Wilderness	Preaches and dies in Moab
Shepherd				Savior				
40 Years of Exile				40 Years of Leadership				
Humility				Service				
Midian				Wilderness				
1485–1445 B.C. (40–80 yrs.)				1445–1405 B.C. (80–120 yrs.)				

A Glimpse of the Greatness of God

(Read: Exodus 1-2)

Imagine you are an Israelite—an enslaved Hebrew in the land of Egypt. You have just read the decree of Pharaoh, the king: "Every boy that is born you must throw into the river, but let every girl live" (Exod. 1:22).

A horrifying edict—utterly shocking. But even worse, you discover that your wife is now pregnant. She will bear a child— soon. If the baby is a girl, well enough. Life is difficult as a slave, but she will survive. But if your wife delivers a newborn boy he must be immediately destroyed or your whole family will face death.

When the day of delivery at last arrives, there is an even deeper agony than the physical trauma of childbirth. In the hearts of both you and your wife rests an unasked question—an unthinkable thought.

What if it's a boy?

"It's a boy."

What do you do now?

If you are Amram and Jochebed, the parents of Moses, you push back your fear, praise God for a beautiful son and take immediate measures to protect him. "By faith Moses' parents hid him for three months after he was born, because they saw he was no ordinary child, and they were not afraid of the king's edict" (Heb. 11:23).

God had a task for Moses, a vast and monumental work years in the future for which God would uniquely prepare him. But that preparation had to begin with the faith of Moses' parents. For the remainder of his life, Moses could look back on the bedrock faith of his mother and father who, though facing the threat of death, chose to stand in awe of the invisible God rather than in awe of an earthly king.

What a challenge to parents and parents-to-be. Are you allowing your deep faith in God to be used as a vital part of God's preparation process for your child? How are you demonstrating to your little ones the fact that your trust in God outweighs any and every earthly circumstance? Your child's first glimpse of God will be through *your eyes.* What will that glimpse reveal?

Rewarding the faith of Moses' parents, God arranged for their infant son to be adopted by none other than the daughter of

Pharaoh. In one of those beautiful twists of irony that God so delights to use, the princess selected Moses' own mother to nurse him and raise him until he was old enough to enter training in the courts of Pharaoh.

But prior to his education in the premier Egyptian universities, Moses learned the ways of God and the history of his people at the knee of Jochebed, his mother. How patiently and consistently this couple of faith must have instructed their young son. Knowing that he would soon be plunged into the world of royalty and idolatry, Amram and Jochebed instilled in Moses the fear of the one God, and a deep love for God's people. This is borne out in Heb. 11:25 where Moses is said to have chosen "to be mistreated along with the people of Israel rather than to enjoy the pleasures of sin for a short time."

When Moses, in the prime of his manhood, was called upon to make a value judgment that would affect his entire future, he did not look to his peers or his education as a guiding star. Turning his back on a potential career at the crest of world power and culture, Moses chose instead to identify with a despised people and an "unknown" God. "He regarded disgrace for the sake of Christ as of greater value than the treasures of Egypt, because he was looking ahead to his reward. By faith he left Egypt, not fearing the king's anger; he persevered because he saw him who is invisible" (Heb. 11:26,27).

Why *shouldn't* Moses have feared the king's anger? Everyone else in the world feared the wrath of Pharaoh. But not Moses. Why? Because planted in the back of this man's mind was an indelible memory. His own mother and father—even in the face of death—"were not afraid of the king's edict." Instead, they deliberately chose to trust the God of Israel. So would Moses!

This is a phenomenal testimony to the impact of godly parents on a young child. How long was Moses actually under the influence of his real mother and father? Until he was weaned? At age five, perhaps? Even if Jochebed was retained as a nurse until Moses reached early adolescence, consider the impact she made on her son's life. At the age of 40, when Moses faced a major crossroads, the simple values instilled by his Hebrew mother when he was still a young child outweighed the influence of a prestigious education in the finest schools and universities of his day! Moses chose for God. Moses chose for Israel. Moses chose disgrace, danger and possible death over the hollow rewards of materialism, sensuality, fame and power. Through the eyes of Amram and Jochebed, he had caught a glimpse of the greatness of God and not even the golden lure of imperial Egypt could persuade him to turn away.

In an era today of "career-minded" parents, round-the-clock child care centers and "television babysitting," Moses' parents provide a critical reminder: The consistent, loving influence of godly parents in the early years of a child's life has an immeasurable impact on the value system that will guide that child throughout later life. The first glimpse of God through the eyes of mother and father may be the most significant glimpse of all.

A Glimpse of the Grace of God

(Read: Exodus 3-4)

The Bible does not reveal when the heart of young Moses began to incline toward his despised, enslaved people. How many nights must he have brooded along the broad, moonlit Nile, contemplating his true roots? How often had he winced as the whip of an Egyptian taskmaster cracked across the bare back of a Hebrew workman? Had he ever dreamed of charging to the rescue of his countrymen in a gleaming chariot, scattering the Egyptians in panic and leading his people forth in triumph?

Perhaps. But here, Scripture is silent. The account simply says that "he saw an Egyptian beating a Hebrew, one of his own people. Glancing this way and that and seeing no one, he killed the Egyptian and hid him in the sand" (Exod. 2:11,12).

At the age of 40, Moses became a murderer—a marked man. His rash, violent action severed all ties to his previous way of life and thrust him into the role of Israel's deliverer and champion. There was only one problem: Israel wasn't ready for a deliverer and champion—least of all Moses. Acts 7:25 says that "Moses thought his own people would realize that God was using him to rescue them, but they did not." If Moses had been expecting an open-arms, strike-up-the-band welcome, he was bitterly disappointed.

Overnight, the heir to the throne became a fugitive from justice. His own people didn't want him. Nothing had turned out the way he had planned. His dreams lay broken and trampled in the dust.

So Moses ran.

What might have been the thoughts of the exiled prince as he crossed the lonely wilderness?

But God—look what I gave up to identify with my people and leave royalty behind me. Look what I sacrificed to turn my back on the gods of Egypt and follow You. And now look—I'm a fugitive! No family. No country. What's to become of me?

Nevertheless, the faith of Moses held firm. "By faith . . . he persevered because he saw him who is invisible" (Heb. 11:27).

Encountering the daughters of Jethro as he rested by a well in the desolate land of Midian, Moses moved into a new phase of life. The Exodus account says that Moses "was content to dwell" with Jethro (Exod. 2:21 KJV). "Content" is an adequate translation of the Hebrew; he was content, but not altogether happy. He was still an alien—a foreigner—and he knew it.

So Moses traded in his princely robes for the homespun garb of a shepherd, the promise of a golden scepter for a wooden staff, his royal companions for a flock of sheep. And for the next 40 years, the man who could have been king of Egypt would wander in obscurity through the desert valleys of Midian. Moses the "powerful in speech and action" (Acts 7:22) would become Moses the simple herdsman, Moses the unknown. And he had every reason to believe his life would be no different until the day he died.

But then he caught a glimpse of God. And life could no longer be the same.

While Moses listened to the bleating of his flock in the desert, God's ears were tuned to a different sound back in the land of Egypt.

"The Israelites groaned in their slavery and cried out, and their cry for help because of their slavery went up to God" (Exod. 2:23).

God heard His people; He remembered His covenant with Abraham, Isaac and Jacob. And the cries of His people tugged at the very heart of God. *It was time now.* Time for Israel to be set free, to enter into their inheritance. And it was time to raise up a leader to gather the people and lead them out.

Hundreds of miles away, a bush in the desert of Midian burst into flames. An unrelated incident? Not from God's perspective. Because about that time Moses "happened" by. And the bush kept on burning. And burning. But it wasn't consumed. As Moses drew near to investigate, he had no idea he was walking into one of the greatest crossroads of his life.

The voice of God called to Moses from the flames.

"I have seen the misery of my people in Egypt. I have heard them crying out . . . and I am concerned about their suffering . . . . So now, go. I am sending you to Pharaoh to bring my people the Israelites out of Egypt" (Exod. 3:7,10).

What must have gone through the old shepherd's mind at that moment?

Who, ME? Moses the fugitive? At one time I might have considered . . . when I was young . . . when I was a prince . . . but now? Why, I'm just a weather-beaten old shepherd.

Years earlier, Moses had tried to rescue his people (Acts 7:25). And he had been the right man, in the right place, with the right motive . . . at the wrong time! God had neither commissioned nor empowered Moses to do what he had done. As a result, his reckless action brought only harm and pain . . . without freeing a single Hebrew.

But now God was calling the would-be leader out of retirement— *40 years later.* Moses had been stripped of the external trappings of power and authority, stripped of his pride in education, title and youthful vigor. And just as the 80-year-old shepherd was contemplating retirement in Midian, God said, "Moses, I have a job tailor-made for you. It is time to return to Egypt, for you're My man to lead the Israelites out of bondage."

In this, Moses' second glimpse of God, he saw a God of grace. A God who not only remembered the anguish of His people back in Egypt, but also the discarded dreams of a discouraged servant. Moses had wanted so much to do something for God. Tried so hard. And failed so miserably. But God hadn't written him off as an impetuous bumbler— a hopeless case. Instead, He sent Moses to school. The former prince was a *summa cum laude* graduate of Egypt's best institutions. But God said, "Come into the desert with Me, Moses. I want to teach you something your instructors in Egypt knew nothing about. I want to teach you how to wait on God—how to live in dependence on Me.''

Moses thought he was on the shelf. Not true. He was actually in a desert classroom with God as his sole Professor. It was a long course of study—*40 years*. But when Moses was ready to graduate God presented his diploma at the burning bush.

Do you feel shelved by God? Have you ever entertained feelings that God might have used you in the past but then you made some mistakes . . . and God has passed you by? Perhaps you need a fresh glimpse of the God of grace.

Moses' crime was *murder*—remember that. As he wandered through the barren hills of Midian with his sheep, he must have relived the painful incident many times.

If only I hadn't killed him! If only I had waited. If only I had consulted the Lord before I jumped in with both feet. Think what the Lord might have been able to do through my life . . . .

It was true. Moses had made a dreadful, costly mistake. And he could not call back that action; he could not undo what he had done. Moses was reaping a bitter harvest for the violence he had sown, and he would continue to reap it for years.

But Moses was dead wrong about one thing: He imagined God could no longer use him. Because of his past, he saw himself as permanently set aside, totally washed up in terms of service for God.

And then . . . a bush caught fire in Midian. And God spoke Moses' name. And God gave him a job to do.

A Glimpse of the Glory of God

(Read: Exodus 32-33)

The scene shifts.

It is some months later on a mountainside where a life and death drama is unfolding.

Israel had absolutely no idea of the danger she was facing. Only one man stood between an entire nation and utter oblivion. And that one man had good reason to step aside and let destruction rush in like a flood.

Moses and his young aide Joshua were high on the craggy peaks of Mt. Sinai. While Joshua waited some distance away, Moses was in conference with the God of Israel, receiving from God's hand the commandments that were to guide the nation's life as they moved into the land of promise.

But no sooner had Moses received the tablets than the voice of God stopped him in his tracks. Something was wrong—terribly wrong in the Israelite camp at the base of the mountain. While Moses had been with God, the people down below had broken all bonds of restraint and had plunged into an idolatrous orgy. With Aaron's help, they had fashioned a golden calf, proclaiming *it* to be the god who brought them up out of Egypt. After bowing before this image and offering sacrifice, the people indulged themselves in a huge, riotous party that was now completely out of control.

One can well imagine that Moses was as close as he would ever want to be to the awesome wrath of a holy God.

The Lord told Moses, " 'I have seen these people and they are a stiff-necked people. *Now leave me alone so that my anger may burn against them and that I may destroy them.* Then I will make you into a great nation' " (Exod. 32:9,10, italics added).

On the one side, a nation of perhaps two million men, women and children. On the other side, an angry God ready to destroy them all.

In between—one man: Moses.

After all the grief the rebellious Israelites had put him through, Moses might easily have stepped to one side. "That's right, Lord. Give those rebels what they deserve. Let them have it!"

But Moses didn't do that. Instead, he immediately "sought the favor of the Lord his God." Moses prayed for his people—earnestly, fervently, persuasively.

Result? "The Lord relented and did not bring on his people the disaster he had threatened" (Exod. 32:14).

But the crisis wasn't over. Even after God had administered severe discipline (Exod. 32:27-35) a dark, threatening cloud of apprehension hovered over the camp.

Once again the voice of God spoke to a troubled Moses: " 'Leave this place, you and the people you brought up out of Egypt, and go to the land I promised on oath to Abraham, Isaac and Jacob . . . I will send an angel before you and drive out the Canaanites, Amorites, Hittites, Perizzites, Hivites and Jebusites. Go up to the land flowing with milk and honey. *But I will not go with you,* because you are a stiff-necked people and I might destroy you on the way' " (Exod. 33:1-3).

Was that so bad? The land would be theirs; the milk and honey would be theirs. A mighty angelic being would go before them, easily capable of dealing with any and every enemy they might encounter. Why not pack up and get started . . . ?

Moses wasn't moving. Not so much as an inch. If God wasn't going to Canaan, then neither was he. If God would not lead the way for Israel, then Israel wasn't about to budge, if Moses could help it. If the Lord would not be in their midst, then nothing was worthwhile anyway. It wasn't the *land of God* Moses was concerned about—it was the *God of the land.* No matter if an army of angels was sent to accompany them; what Moses wanted was the presence of his Lord.

What follows is one of the most amazing conversations ever recorded between God and man (Exod. 33:12-23). The broken-hearted servant of God had gone through so much with the Lord at his side that he would not be denied that precious companionship. Moses had learned well the lesson of dependence. He would not proceed without the positive assurance that God would go with him. "Teach me your ways so that I may know you," he prayed.

The Lord replied, "My Presence will go with you, and I will give you rest" (Exod. 33:12,13).

How could Moses ask for more reassurance than that? He had God's personal pledge. But still Moses waited.

The responsibilities were so awesome, the weight of leadership so heavy that the heart of Moses longed for even more assurances, even greater revelation.

"If your Presence does not go with us, do not send us up from here," he prayed. "How will anyone know that you are pleased with me and with your people unless you go with us? What else will distinguish me and your people from all the other people on the face of the earth?" (Exod. 33:15,16).

God was not angry or impatient with Moses. Instead, He gave him additional words of assurance (Exod. 33:17).

But *still* Moses waited.

"Then Moses said, 'Now show me your glory' " (Exod. 33:18).

And God did precisely that (Exod. 33:19-23). Taking special precautions to prevent Moses from being consumed by the brilliance of His glory, the Lord gave him an unforgettable glimpse of Himself.

When Israel's aged leader finally climbed back down the mountain to rejoin his people, his face shone with the supernatural radiance of what he had seen. Moses had been with God; there was no doubt about that.

What can be learned from this unusual exchange between God and Moses? Take a few minutes to reflect on your own prayer life. Perhaps just this morning you mumbled the words, "Lord, be with me today," as you stepped out your front door and plunged into your day. If someone were to question you more closely on what you had prayed, you might have cited Scripture passages like Hebrews 13:5, where the Lord says, "Never will I leave you; never will I forsake you."

You know the Scriptures; you know God's promises. But are those words of God only words to you today, or are they gripping certainties? Is the active, personal presence of Jesus Christ in your life some vague, mystical concept, or is it a clear, in-focus reality? It's one thing to give passive intellectual assent to the promises of God: "Oh, sure, God is with me—the Bible says so." But it's something else to be able to cry out from the depths of your spirit, "I *know* Jesus Christ is with me, right now. I *know* that He has a handle on every situation I face. I *know* that He is leading the way in my life today."

That kind of heart-felt confidence doesn't come cheaply. Like any other meaningful relationship, a walk with God takes a significant investment of time—quality time. Sometimes it may mean carving minutes out of an already heavy schedule to pore over the Scriptures. Sometimes it may mean lingering in prayer until your mind is able to sort through the distractions and get a firm hold on spiritual realities.

Moses lingered in prayer until the glow of God's presence

burned in his soul like fire and shone from his face like the sun. And everyone knew that this man had been with God.

Moses was hungry for closer communication with God. Not satisfied with merely knowing God's words, he craved to know God's ways. He longed to behold God's glory. And God said, "There's never been anyone like this man, Moses. I can speak with him just like a man talks to his friend."

Take some time this week to evaluate your personal goals. Then stack them alongside Moses' goal to know the Almighty God "face to face." How do your goals measure up to *that* goal? Could it be that you need to prayerfully rearrange your priorities . . . your schedule?

It might not be as rugged a task as it first appears. Remember, Moses had to climb a mountain to meet with God. All you have to do is speak His Name.

He's that close.

God delights in enjoying the company of His people, even if only for two or three minutes a day. But one principle remains unchanged in our age of time-saving technology: *Spirituality comes from spending time in the presence of the Lord.* "Anyone who comes to him must believe that he exists and that he rewards those who earnestly seek him" (Heb. 11:6). It was true in the days of Moses; it was true in the days of David and of Paul. And it is true today.

The words of Christ in Matthew 7:7 are literally translated, *"Keep on asking* and it shall be given to you; *keep on seeking* and you shall find; *keep on knocking* and it shall be opened to you.

Glimpses of God really aren't all that unusual. But it's a sure bet you'll never have one . . . if you never look.

Work It Through

1. Read Hebrews 11:23-39 and discuss the critical major decision that Moses made concerning his future. What would that choice have meant to his career? . . . his material possessions? . . . his future security? What was it that gave Moses strength during this difficult period of his life?

_____

_____

2. Read Stephen's overview of the life of Moses in Acts 7:17-42. Did Moses intend to break with Egypt at the age of 40, or was his murder of the Egyptian simply a "crime of passion" that suddenly thrust him into the role of a deliverer?

_____

_____

3. When God spoke to Moses from the burning bush and commissioned him to lead the Israelites out of Egypt, the old shepherd seemed preoccupied with his own failures and limitations. Was Moses' "humility" before God a spiritual response? Why or why not?

_____

_____

4. It seems as though God would have become impatient with Moses for refusing to lead the Israelites until Moses "nailed down" the absolute assurance that God would go with His people (Exod. 33:1-23). Didn't Moses' repeated protests reveal a lack of faith on his part? Why did God seem to be pleased to allow His servant to "win the argument"? What principles from this incident might we carry over into our own prayer lives?

_____

_____

NOTES

Introduction to

Samuel

Early risers, camped at the edge of a mountain lake, have the edge on everyone else.

Theirs is that first cup of coffee in the morning. Not ordinary, mortal stuff, but the kind perked to steaming perfection over a snapping campfire.

Theirs is the hesitant light of a new day, the cool silence of the forest.

And theirs is the mist, curling from the surface of the lake, vanishing as soon as it rises.

Watching mist can be a profound experience, for the Bible says your life is a mist. Rising for a moment in the sun, then gone. Appearing only to disappear.

The world says, since life is slipping away, live as much of it as you can for yourself. Cram pleasure into every fading minute. But God says, since life on earth is brief and temporary, live it for eternity. Entrust your life to Me, and I'll give it meaning that will outlast time itself.

Do you want your life to have eternal significance? Then read on . . . and meet Samuel, a man who can show you the way.

Samuel's LIFE IN SUMMARY

Preparation for Ministry
(1 Samuel 1:1-4:1a)

*A*s the turbulent period of the judges draws to a close, God blesses a man named Elkanah and his barren wife Hannah with a son. The child Samuel, "asked of God," is consecrated to the Lord from birth. In fulfillment of a vow, Hannah brings Samuel to Shiloh where he begins his life of godly service under the tutoring of Eli the priest.

Through Samuel, God delivers a shocking message of judgment upon Eli's household for Eli's failure to deal with the blatant immorality of his sons. Careful to both hear and declare the word of the Lord, Samuel is soon established as a prophet throughout all of Israel.

Persevering in the Ministry
(1 Samuel 4:1b-7:2)

*W*hile still a young man, Samuel sees the terrible fulfillment of the prophetic word he spoke to Eli. Israel's army suffers a devastating defeat by the Philistines at Aphek, both of Eli's sons perish in battle, and the ark of God falls into enemy hands. Hearing the news, Eli collapses and dies.

For a period of 20 years, Scripture is silent on Samuel's activities. Already recognized as a man of God and a prophet, Samuel works behind the scenes proclaiming God's word and providing moral leadership for the people.

Focus	Preparation for Ministry (1 Samuel 1:1–4:1a)				Persevering in the Ministry (1 Samuel 4:1b–7:2)
Divisions	His birth an answer to prayer	His dedication to the Lord	His ministry before the Lord	His call; established as a prophet	20 years behind the scenes
Topics	Servant of the Priest				Servant of the Lord
	Under Authority				Growing Authority
	"Asked of God"				Taught by God
Place	Ramah/Shiloh				All Israel
Approx. Dates (Age)	1100–1088 B.C. (Birth–12 yrs.)				1087–1076 (13–25 yrs.)

Public Ministry
(1 Samuel 7:3-7:17)

*L*ike Moses emerging from the wilderness to lead his people, Samuel makes a dramatic entrance into a public ministry following 20 years or more "behind the scenes."

The Israelites, weary of Philistine domination and ready to seek the Lord, turn to Samuel who in turn points the way to repentance and national revival. He prays earnestly for the people as they gather at Mizpah, then watches as God throws back an enemy attack, breaking the Philistine stranglehold on the nation. Samuel continues to serve the people as prophet, priest, and judge, making a regular 200-mile circuit from his home base at Ramah.

Personal Ministry
(1 Samuel 8:1-25:1)

*A*s Samuel grows older, he appoints his sons as judges over Israel—men who are morally unfit for the office. Chafing under such corrupt spiritual leadership, Israel's leaders demand a king that they might be "like all the nations."

Grieved at heart, Samuel warns them of the consequences, but follows God's instructions and anoints Saul. When the new king refuses to obey God's commands, Samuel is forced to confront him with a sentence of divine judgment. Eventually, God leads Samuel to anoint a new king—young David—one of Samuel's final acts as judge over God's people.

Public Ministry (1 Samuel 7:3–7:17)			Personal Ministry (1 Samuel 8:1–25:1)				
Leads Israel back to God	Leads Israel to victory over Philistines	Summary: Samuel's work as a judge	Failure of his sons; people demand a king	Anoints Saul; installs him as king	Brings words of judgment to Saul	Anoints David	Dies in Ramah
Spokesman to the People			Spokesman to the King				
Peak of Authority			Declining Authority				
Taught for God			Rebuked by God				
Circuit Ministry (home base, Ramah)			Circuit Ministry (home base, Ramah)				
1076–1050 (25–50 yrs.)			1050–1020 (50–death)				

Listen for God's Will

(Read: 1 Samuel 3:1-10)

Sometime during the night, a voice spoke to the boy in his bed near the ark of God.

"Samuel! Samuel!"

Samuel heard the words, understood that he was being summoned, but did not recognize the voice.

It happened to be the voice of God. But Samuel was still a child—he "did not yet know the LORD." So he mistook the call of God for the call of his guardian, old Eli the priest. Three times Samuel obediently responded to what he thought was Eli's summons. Finally, the priest understood. He told his young helper what to do if the voice called again.

"So Samuel went and lay down in his place.

"The LORD came and stood there, calling as at other times, 'Samuel! Samuel!'

"Then Samuel said, 'Speak, for your servant is listening' " (Sam. 3:9,10).

Scripture says that the Word of the Lord was "precious" (1 Sam. 3:1 KJV) in those waning days of the judges. In other words, no one knew where to find it. No one was seeing visions; no one was dreaming dreams; and if there were any burning bushes in those days, they were the kind that caught fire and burned to ashes.

No wonder it took Eli so long to get the message. "Maybe Someone *is* calling him. But it wouldn't be . . . it couldn't be . . . ."

Eli ministered every day of his life in "the tent of meeting." As he went about his duties he often stood within inches of the Ark of God—the very place God said He would manifest His presence. *Strange that the last thing in the world Eli expected to hear was the voice of God.*

Can you put yourself in Samuel's place? There you are, lying on your bed, heart churning, knowing the very next sound you hear may be the voice of Almighty God.

Yet when God called to Samuel again, the boy was ready with his answer. "Your servant is listening!" You've got my full attention, Lord. I'm ready to hear . . . and obey.

What would you give to have an experience like that? Conversation with the Creator of the Universe! Can you imagine what it would be like to pick up the phone, dial "H" for heaven and get the Almighty on the line? Not some canned dial-a-prayer, but *God Himself!* With God on the line, chances are you'd be ready to do some serious listening.

God's audible voice . . . at your bedside . . . talking to you in a clear, understandable way. But that was way back then. In the old days. He doesn't speak that way anymore, does he? And even in Samuel's day, He didn't speak to everyone who longed to hear Him. Only a few were so privileged in the Old Testament. A Moses, a Gideon . . . and hundreds of years later, a Samuel. And those men could never be sure *when* He was going to speak, of *if* He would speak to them again.

Here you are today, wanting so much to hear God's voice. Wanting so much to get His perspective on this confusing, complex world you live in. Needing His encouragement, His counsel, His guidance through the corridors of your daily life. Where can you turn to hear His voice today? What would His bedside conversation be with you? Perhaps it would be this:

"You already have My Word! You already have My encouragement and counsel and advice. I gave it to you—it's yours. Why don't you pick it up and read it?"

You may already own three or four copies of the book known as "the Word of God." The Word of God! Could it be that the truth is so close, you have looked right past it? Could it be that the abundance of Bibles occupying shelves, pulpits, and nightstands has caused its message to be overlooked?

Shake yourself loose from all the old cliches about the Bible for a minute and lock your mind like a vise around these truths:

The Bible is God's Word. One hundred percent of it. And it's His Word to you. Personally. Everything you need to know about Him, everything you need to understand about living the Christian life is contained between its covers.

The Holy Spirit is available to you, right now, to be your Teacher. He longs to take that written Word and make it alive and powerful in your heart. Contemplate that for a moment. Perhaps you think of Samuel as a privileged man because God spoke to him in an audible voice. But how often did God speak to him that way? Ten times? A hundred times? And yet, you have the privilege of hearing God speak directly to your needs every minute of the day!

If you lack the Word of God in your life, it is only because you choose to lack the Word of God.

If your life is empty, confused, fearful, or without direction, it is only because you have decided to let it become that way.

It doesn't have to be. Help is as close as the pages of that familiar Book. Why not find a quiet corner somewhere right now, open up His mighty Word, and invite Him to turn your life upside down? Let that ancient prayer of a wise little boy be your prayer, too:

"Speak Lord, for your servant is listening."

Be Obedient in the Hard Tasks

(Read: 1 Samuel 3:11-21)

There are few people in the world who could honestly say, "I grew up in a perfect home." There was never any tension, never any strife, never any heartache. Even those raised in a Christian environment would be hard-pressed to make a statement like that. Because homes are filled with people—imperfect people—people with rough edges. And when rough edges brush against one another, there is bound to be friction.

You'd think Samuel's homelife would have been different, somehow. After all, he was raised in the home of a priest. And not just *any* priest, but the spiritual leader of the nation Israel. Seems like that ought to count for something. Even the name of Samuel's boyhood home—Shiloh—meant "the peaceful one."

But there was woefully little peace. Eli's sons, Hophni and Phinehas, grew up to become hardened, godless rebels. By contrast, Samuel "ministered before the Lord under Eli" and "the LORD was with Samuel" (1 Sam. 3:1,19).

Do you see the potential for friction? Samuel, the "foster brother" of Hophni and Phinehas, joins the family at age three and grows up doing everything right. Eli loves him, the people of Israel love him, God richly blesses him. Result: sibling rivalry, resentment, and ultimately hatred. As Hophni and Phinehas grew older, they became more and more rebellious, more and more daring in their wickedness, while Samuel grew more godly and dedicated in his service for the Lord.

Can you imagine the charged atmosphere around the dinner table? How difficult it must have been for sensitive young Samuel as he sought to serve Eli and live for the Lord.

As Eli and his boys drifted further and further apart, picture the love relationship that must have been building between the old priest and his earnest young helper, Samuel. While Eli's sons used their father's office to promote their own greed and lust, Samuel brought honor and respect to Shiloh. While Hophni and Phinehas ignored their father's words and scoffed at his counsel, Samuel couldn't get enough teaching—couldn't be more eager to obey. The two sons of Eli cared nothing for the LORD but the young son of Hannah and Elkanah loved Him deeply. How encouraging the boy's companionship must have been to the priest. What a joy in the midst of so many heavy anxieties and heartaches!

For Samuel, the old priest was mother and father and teacher all rolled up into one. Together they opened the door of the house of the Lord to welcome the worshippers. Together they closed the gates at evening, reflecting on the day's activities as the altar fire burned down into softly glowing embers.

That's what made it so difficult—so agonizingly painful when the LORD spoke Eli's doom into young Samuel's ear. A bitter message of judgment devoid of the faintest hint of hope. Because Eli had not restrained his sons from dragging the name of the Lord through the mud of their sins, the house of Eli faced swift, terrible discipline. There could be no atonement or sacrifice for their sins.

How do you deliver that kind of message to someone you love? How do you look into those familiar old eyes, so full of sadness already, and pronounce God's judgment?

Little wonder that as Samuel opened the gates after what must have been a sleepless night "he was afraid to tell Eli the vision" (1 Sam. 3:15). Nevertheless, when the old man confronted his helper, asking to hear what the Lord had said, Samuel resisted the temptation to soften the blow, or paraphrase God's judgment. Scripture says that "Samuel told him everything, hiding nothing from him" (1 Sam. 3:18).

And when the Lord saw that Samuel could be trusted with even a heartbreaking task like this, He did not hesitate to place more and more authority into Samuel's hands. He began to use the young man as His spokesman to a whole generation.

What hard assignment are you facing right now? Sometimes it involves going to another person and asking for forgiveness. That's never easy. But even more difficult, it may mean going personally to face a person who has offended *you.* Jesus gives clear instructions in Matthew 18:15-17. If someone hurts you, if someone gossips behind your back and you become aware of it, you are to "go and show him his fault, just between the two of you." You're not to go to someone else; you're not to complain to your friends; and, at this point, you're not to report it to your minister. Jesus said you need to deal with the person who hurt you. Face to face. Openly and honestly. And that's hard.

Who do you need to see this week? Who do you need to pick up the phone and call? Are you willing to do that difficult assignment in God's strength? Remember, if you refuse to obey Him in one area of your life, you may forfeit the important ministry God has been wanting to place in your hands.

God is looking for Samuels today. Men and women who are hungry to serve, and prepared to do His will.

Even when it hurts.

Be a Ready Vessel

(Read: 1 Samuel 7: 2-17)

In the days of the American Revolution, a group of citizens banded together to form what would become a historic militia. Each man—whether a farmer, tinker, lawyer, or blacksmith— went about his normal daily routine, but with this difference: When the signal went out indicating trouble, these men became soldiers. Always ready with powder and shot, musket and pack, they could drop whatever they were doing and become an effective fighting force in a matter of minutes.

That's why they were called *Minutemen.* When the alarm sounded they didn't need to rummage through attics looking for mess kits. ("Marge, have you seen my canteen?") They didn't need to sit down for half an hour to clean their guns. ("Where in the world did I leave those musket balls?") Wherever the minutemen were, whether hoeing the corn patch or presenting a case to the jury, they were only seconds from being soldiers.

God is looking for Minutemen today. Men and women who are ready—on a moment's notice—to follow the Commander's signal and step into whatever situation He sets before them.

Samuel was God's Minuteman throughout his long, fruitful life. Nowhere is that more evident that in 1 Samuel 7. After 20 years under the thumb of Philistine domination, Israel was ready to repent and turn back to the God of their fathers. It was their own sin and rebellion that had brought them to grief.

Because they had forsaken the Lord, He allowed them to suffer under the hateful heel of their enemies.

The Ark of the Covenant, once the reassuring symbol of God's presence and blessing, had been absent for *two decades*. In its place, grotesque images of Baal and Ashtoreth dotted the landscape.

At last, Israel understood. Chapter 7, verse 2 says they "mourned and sought after the LORD." Troubled and heavy-hearted, they were ready to repent of their pride, worldliness, and ungodly lifestyle. They wanted the Lord.

But where could they go to find Him? Shiloh was a shattered ruin. Weeds grew up through the abandoned altar. The Ark of God was nowhere to be found. Who could they turn to as the source of God's voice for a searching generation?

A nation of people might have perished in despair. But God had a Minuteman: Samuel the faithful; Samuel, the man who walked with God.

When tragedy tears at the lives of your neighbors, do they know whose door to knock on for guidance and counsel? Do the people where you work know who to come to when their lives hit bottom and they can't find answers?

When shipwreck strikes, desperate swimmers look for an island—a rock. Are lost men and women swimming for your shore, groping for the meaning that sustains you? Or do they know anything about your faith . . . your commitment . . . your Savior? Samuel's countrymen knew! Through 20 years of idolatry in Israel, Samuel stood firm in his commitment to God. Though no one else cared for the things of God, though no one else worried about personal purity or the Word of the Lord, or prayer and sacrifice—Samuel did. Like a Minuteman, he stayed ready—musket clean, powder dry. His life was a clean vessel, ready to be thrust into service at a moment's notice. And when the hearts of his countrymen were tender toward spiritual things, Samuel was God's man for the moment. On the scene. Ready to counsel. Ready to pray.

If God threw open a door of opportunity to you before you finished reading this page, would you be ready to seize it? Ready to witness, ready to counsel, ready to comfort and encourage . . . does that describe your life?

Or would you have to take care of some overdue details first? Some unconfessed sins, some selfish attitudes, some bitter feelings against a brother or sister in Christ?

Imagine a Minuteman who had to stop and mend his pack or buy his supplies before he could join his comrades in battle. Before he ever reached the field of battle, the issue would be settled, one way or the other. It's the same for followers of the Lord of Hosts. If you desire more than anything else to be used of God, then you need to be ready: walking in the Spirit, sins confessed, personal relationships yielded to His control, prepared to do battle with the razor-sharp sword of His Word.

In 2 Chronicles 16:9 (KJV), you'll read these words: "The eyes of the LORD run to and fro throughout the whole earth, to show Himself strong in the behalf of them whose heart is perfect toward Him."

Read that verse again. Do you see what God is saying? You don't have to plead and beg to be used by God. He is *looking* right now across the face of the earth for someone to be His Minuteman. His eyes search every city and town, every home and family. At this very moment, His eyes are searching your life, your heart.

The question is not, "Does God want to use me?" He does! The question is, "Am I a ready vessel for His service?" Though the requirements are stringent to become one of God's Minutemen, the "enlistment quotas" are unlimited. There is always room for one more. Why not join Samuel's faithful ranks today?

Work It Through

1. Review the chart of Samuel's life. What unhappy parallel can you see between the life of Eli and the life of Samuel? How might it have paid long-range dividends if these two godly men had cut short their "public ministry" time in favor of "home ministry" time?

_____

_____

_____

2. Samuel enjoyed the incredible experience of actually hearing the audible voice of God. In what sense is the Christian's experience with "God's voice" even *preferable* to Samuel's situation?

_____

_____

_____

3. One of Samuel's first prophetic assignments came when he was just a boy: It was the difficult task of "speaking the truth in love" to Eli, his beloved foster-father. Surface the key principles from Matthew 18:15–17 in regard to solving difficult personal relationship problems.

_____

_____

_____

4. Why was Samuel compared to a "Minuteman"? What practical steps could you take to insure that you will be "God's Minuteman" this week?

_____

_____

_____

NOTES

NOTES

Saul

Pressure. It's as American as cheeseburgers and the Super Bowl. You go to bed with it, you wake up with it, and in some cases you sit up with it all night long.

Pressure. It's the lifeblood of the antacid and tranquilizer industries. No matter who you are or where you are, more than likely you're struggling with increasing pressure in your life.

What kinds of pressure? All kinds. The pressure to conform to an increasingly sensual society; the pressure to make financial ends meet in the face of runaway inflation; family pressure; school pressure; peer pressure; church pressure; the pressure to succeed; the pressure to be popular.

The real question in coping with pressure is not whether you will face pressure (you will), but rather how you will *handle* the pressures you already face. How you will deal with them on a daily basis.

The same wind that overturns one sailboat propels another toward its destination. The difference lies neither in the wind nor in the boat, but in the way the sails are set. To some people, pressure is always negative, always distressing. To others, a very similar set of circumstances may prove to be a creative force leading to the release of new power, new dynamic, new joy.

The life of Saul, Israel's first king, is a classic portrait of a man under pressure. A closer look at his life will reveal two destructive— but very human—responses to the crunch of circumstances. It will also demonstrate that God can equip you to deal with pressing situations in a way that will draw you ever closer to Himself.

The King Selected
(1 Sam. 9-12)

*B*ecause Samuel's sons prove to be unjust and corrupt judges, the elders of Israel demand that Samuel make them a king "like all the nations."

In response to these demands, God sends Samuel to anoint Saul, the tall, good-looking son of a wealthy Benjamite farmer. Initially humble and restrained, Saul seems to be an ideal choice for Israel's first king. God's Spirit descends upon Saul in a mighty way and the young man confirms his kingship by rallying Israel.

As all of Israel gathers for a great celebration at Gilgal to confirm Saul as king, Samuel steps forward to make his farewell speech. The old prophet makes it clear that Saul is the king of **their** choice— they have chosen Saul rather than God as their king. Yet if Israel and its king agree to obey the Lord, all will be well. If, on the other hand, they rebel, Samuel issues this stern warning: "If you persist in doing evil, both you and your king will be swept away."

Focus	The King Selected (1 Samuel 9–11)				
Divisions	A tall, impressive young man; Saul grows up on his father's farm	Saul anointed by Samuel	Saul made King	Saul rescues Jabesh	Saul confirmed as King
Topics	Victorious in Battle				
	Holy Spirit Upon Him				
	A Good Beginning: Humble				
Place	Gibeah in Benjamin				
Approx. Dates (Age)	1073–1043 B.C. (Birth–30 yrs.)				

The King Rejected
(1 Sam. 13-31)

Despite the clear warning of Samuel, King Saul soon disobeys the Lord's revealed word. Instead of waiting for the prophet to arrive for a ceremony at Gilgal (as previously instructed), Saul takes it upon himself to offer a burnt offering in an attempt to unify the people. As a result of this act, Samuel prophesies that the kingdom of Saul will not continue and that the Lord will seek out a man "after His own heart."

Some time later, Saul again disobeys a specific command by neglecting to utterly destroy the Amalekites and their livestock. Instead, Saul keeps the king alive as a trophy and saves many of the better animals for his own use. Confronting him with this sin, Samuel reveals that the Lord has torn the kingdom from Saul's hands and has given it to another.

In the coming days Saul is troubled by military stalemates and "evil spirits sent from the Lord." When his young armor-bearer, David (already secretly anointed to replace Saul), destroys the Philistine champion in battle and gains the love and respect of Israel, Saul becomes consumed with jealousy. For the remainder of his life Saul unsuccessfully pursues the young man whom God has ordained to follow him on the throne. Finally, the unhappy king who had started out so well takes his own life after being severely wounded in battle.

The King Rejected (Chart 1 of 2) (1 Samuel 13-15)		
Saul's impatience at Gilgal; rebuked by Samuel	Saul makes a rash and foolish vow	Saul disobeys in Amalekite war; rejected as king
Defeated in Battle		
Holy Spirit Departed From Him		
A Terrible Ending: Proud		
Gibeah and Throughout Israel		
1043–1011 B.C. (30–62 yrs.)		

The King Rejected (Chart 2 of 2) (1 Samuel 18-31)		
Saul grows jealous of David; tries to kill him	Saul consults witch	Wounded in battle; takes his own life
Defeated in Battle		
Holy Spirit Departed From Him		
A Terrible Ending: Proud		
Gibeah and Throughout Israel		
1043–1011 B.C. (30–62 yrs.)		

Avoiding the Impatience Trap

(Read: 1 Samuel 13:1–15)

No one plans his own pressures. No one begins the day by saying,

"I think I'll have five or six heavy pressures before lunch today, and then maybe a dozen or so more before I go to bed."

It doesn't happen that way, does it? Pressure builds in much more subtle— and devastating— ways.

The phone rings and you discover a new wrinkle in your evening that upsets all your carefully laid plans.

Thumbing through some papers on your desk, you come across several unpaid bills— at just the moment that your lights go out.

The boss bursts into your office with a life-and-death, hurry-up job that has to be done by 5 o'clock . . . *and done right.*

One of the kids comes down with a serious illness the day you're scheduled to leave on an important business trip.

Pressure comes into your life through a variety of doors and windows, wearing many different disguises. You didn't plan on it, you haven't invited it, you certainly don't *want* it. But there it is. How do you handle it?

In 1 Samuel 13, when Saul rode with 3,000 troops into Israel's hill country, he wasn't expecting a crisis. Really, he wasn't *ready* for a crisis. But what he got was one of the biggest crises of his life.

Coming off a recent victory over the Ammonites, Saul was in no mood for another major confrontation. To make matters worse, there was the frightening sermon by the prophet Samuel just a few days ago. The man of God had actually called down thunder, lightning, and rain from the sky to demonstrate God's displeasure with Israel. Very unnerving!

So the king needed time to think, time to sort things out. He would take a small force into the hills along the Philistine border and organize a defense line. Then he would meet Samuel at Gilgal, keeping an earlier appointment. With Saul at his side, Samuel would offer burnt offerings and fellowship offerings to the Lord on behalf of all the people. Then perhaps together they could seek the Lord's blessings on future military actions.

Saul had it all planned. It was going to be a nice, quiet week.

Then an unexpected guest dropped in . . . *Pressure*.

Saul's valiant son Jonathan had come to the firm opinion that it would be disastrous to allow the Philistine army to establish itself in the southern hill country of Judah. Not one to waste time on formalities, Jonathan leaped into action by leading a surprise attack on a Philistine garrison at Geba (1 Sam. 13:3).

That move caused the Philistine war machine to rumble and roar. Israel became "a stench to the Philistines" (1 Sam. 13:4). The Hebrew word for "stench" is the same word used earlier in the Bible to describe the condition of manna left overnight in a jar. Rotten, rancid, wormy . . . thoroughly disgusting. The Philistines needed no pep talk to get them ready to march on the Israelites.

As Saul assembled the Israelite militia at Gilgal, the "pressure" in the west was growing to awesome proportions:

"The Philistines assembled to fight Israel, with three thousand chariots, six thousand charioteers, and soldiers as numerous as the sand on the seashore" (1 Sam. 13:5).

Goodbye, nice quiet week. Hello, pressure. King Saul now faced a huge, crushing dose of it. How would he cope?

As the relatively inexperienced Hebrew troops gathered at Gilgal for war, a random sample of opinions among the soldiers might have revealed sentiments similar to these:

"If we've got to fight, then let's get at it."

"At least we've got a little momentum going for us since we routed the Ammonites."

"We ought to hit them while we've got the morale, the men, and the tactical advantage."

Certainly that's the way Saul must have viewed the situation. And yet the prophet Samuel had told him to wait seven days at Gilgal (1 Sam. 10:8). *Seven days!* It must have seemed like seven years. Can you visualize yourself in the Israelite camp during that agonizing week of waiting?

The first day slips by, and there's still a little good-natured banter among the men. A lot of talk about the upcoming action. A nagging question: "When are we going to move?" As the days drag on, however, morale begins to ebb as the tension builds. Scattered fights break out in camp over trivial things. Saul dispatches scouts every few hours to scan the horizon for some sign from Samuel. Nothing.

By the start of the sixth day, three-fourths of Saul's army have quietly melted into the surrounding hills. Deserters continue to slip out of camp like air from a leaky tire. And just a few miles away the mighty Philistine army sharpens its swords and prepares to spring.

The sun rises on the seventh day with *still* no word from Samuel. Roll call reveals that Saul's once respectable army has dwindled down to a mere 600 men. Scouts report further movement in the Philistine camp.

Can you imagine the atmosphere in Saul's tent as he continues to wait for Samuel? How would you have handled the situation? How do *you* respond as distressing circumstances crowd into your life to push and tug at your peace of mind? Does pressure drive you closer to the Lord, making you increasingly dependent on Him? Or do your circumstances become stumbling blocks, filling you with dread and fear so that you find yourself farther away from God?

If Saul could have quieted the churning in his soul for a moment, he might have remembered the words of Samuel as the old prophet poured the anointing oil over his head:

"The Spirit of the Lord will come upon you in power . . . you will be changed into a different person . . . . God is with you . . . " (1 Sam. 10:6,7).

He might have recalled that during the days of the judges a farmer's son named Gideon overthrew an army of Midianites so large it was "impossible to count" (Judg. 6:5). Gideon did it with 300 men—half the number of Saul's remaining troops. And he was able to accomplish it because the Lord was with him, just as He was with Saul.

Saul might have recalled many other lessons during those seven days of waiting. If he had placed his trust in God in spite of the circumstances, his descendants might have ruled over Israel throughout all generations (1 Sam. 13:13). But he didn't. Instead of letting the pressure push him into the waiting arms of God, he allowed himself to be swallowed up by feverish impatience. As the sun climbed into the sky on that seventh day, the king decided to take matters into his own hands.

"So he said, 'Bring me the burnt offering and the fellowship offerings.' And Saul offered up the burnt offering" (1 Sam. 13:9).

At that very moment, Samuel strode into camp.

"What have you done?" Samuel demanded.

All of Saul's excuses began to crumble before the old prophet's piercing gaze.

" 'You acted foolishly,' Samuel said. 'You have not kept the command the Lord your God gave you; if you had, he would have established your kingdom over Israel for all time. But now your kingdom will not endure; the Lord has sought out a man after his own heart and appointed him leader of his people, because you have not kept the Lord's command' " (1 Sam. 13:13,14). He knew perfectly well what God had commanded through Samuel. But he allowed the pressure of the moment to determine his actions, rather than the clear word of God.

Saul missed a precious opportunity to confirm his kingship with a resounding declaration of faith in the miracle-working God of Israel. It was an opportunity he could never retrieve. Samuel told him that because of his foolish impatience, his dynasty would be given to another. What might have been Saul's greatest hour of triumph became instead a devastating setback.

Saul had been given God's firm word that Samuel would indeed join him on the seventh day. But the simple fact was Saul didn't trust God to do what He had promised. He didn't really believe God was in control of the situation. From Saul's perspective, things couldn't get any worse. So he listened to the shrill, clamoring voice of circumstance rather than the "still, small voice" (1 Kings 19:12 KJV) of God's Spirit.

What voice are you listening to today? Do you feel like God has placed you in a difficult set of circumstances, then gone off somewhere and forgotten all about you?

If so, you are faced with a choice. You can either choose to allow the pressures in your life to dictate your response; or you can view your pressures as an *opportunity* to prove the strength and faithfulness of God. The apostle Paul chose the latter route, and after his ordeal was over, wrote these revealing words: "We do not want you to be uninformed, brothers, about the hardships we suffered in the province of Asia. *We were under great pressure, far beyond our ability to endure, so that we despaired even of life* . . . But this happened that we might not rely on ourselves but on God . . . He has delivered us from such a deadly peril, and he will deliver us. On him we have set our hope" (2 Cor. 1:8–10).

Only after Paul had come to the end of himself could he begin to discover what the sufficiency of God was all about. Only after he had thoroughly exhausted his own resources could he fully realize the mighty reservoir of God's strength. *"On Him we have set our hope,"* said Paul. Not on our circumstances, not on our ability to cope, not on our talents, not on our education. Our hope is on Him alone.

It's a paradox. You place your hope in Him, and even though your particular situation may or may not change, *the weight is gone.* It rests on His shoulders.

It's like the four-year-old girl who was "helping" her daddy move his library from a downstairs to an upstairs room. The father allowed his helper to carry some paperbacks and magazines up the stairs, then became preoccupied with rearranging the volumes. He was interrupted by the sound of weeping on the stairway. Hurrying out, he discovered his little daughter sitting on the third step with a huge dictionary by her side.

"What's wrong, honey?" her father asked. Between sobs, the little girl told him, "I wanted . . . to help you . . . but this book . . . was too heavy!"

"Here," the man replied. "I've got a solution for that. You just hold onto this book real tight with both hands—got it?" With that, the wise father scooped up his wide-eyed daughter *and* her heavy load and carried them both upstairs. The little girl still held the book—but the father held the little girl.

That's what God wants to do for you. Your situation may be extremely demanding. The weight you carry may seem unbearably heavy. But God has not forgotten you. The One who knows the precise number of hairs on your head is certainly not unaware of your distress. He understands the pressure. And He is waiting to carry both you and your burden if you will place your trust in Him.

Handling Pressure Paralysis
(1 Samuel 17)

Sometimes pressure feels like an annoying *prod*—constantly pushing and poking you into frenzied activity. That's one way it attacks. But there is another, more subtle approach in which pressure creeps alongside and injects you with a dose of *paralysis.*

Just when you need a clear and agile mind the most, the crippling effects of pressure shoot through your system to cloud your vision and numb your brain. Instead of being able to think, decide, move, *act*—all you can do is sit and stare at the wall, or thumb, glassy-eyed, through a magazine you've already read. The higher the level of worry and anxiety, the stiffer your limbs become.

Saul seemed to bounce back and forth between these two very different responses to increasing pressure. At times he was a raging whirlwind of activity: leading armies on wild pursuits through the wilderness, uttering rash vows, venting his jealousy and frustration through outbursts of anger. But as the Israelite army squared off against its Philistine counterpart in the valley of Elah, the troubled king demonstrated that he, too, experienced the debilitating effects of *Pressure Paralysis.*

The Philistines, badly beaten and humiliated at Michmash (1 Sam. 14), had regrouped themselves for another face-off with the hated Israelites. Scripture paints the scene this way: "(The Philistines) pitched camp at Ephes Dammin, between Socoh and Azekah. Saul and the Israelites assembled and camped in the Valley of Elah and drew up their battle line to meet the Philistines. The Philistines occupied one hill and the Israelites another, with the valley between them" (1 Sam. 17:1–3).

Still smarting from their recent defeat, Israel's archenemies were reluctant to launch a bold, frontal attack. Instead, the Philistine war chiefs chose to challenge Saul's forces by means of *representative combat.* This was a fairly common practice in the ancient Near East in which one champion would represent his entire army. Instead of the two armies coming together in combat, two chosen warriors, one from each side, would battle each other to the death. The results of that single conflict could be the major determining factor of "who won the war."

It was always a gamble. But the Philistines had an ace up their sleeve . . . a rather *large* ace named Goliath. If you had to pin the hopes of your army on one individual, then Goliath was definitely the candidate for the job. A warrior from his youth, Goliath was easily nine feet tall in his stocking feet. The coat of bronze armor he wore weighed more than 100 pounds. The iron point of his spear alone weighed 15 pounds. Goliath was the Philistines' "doomsday" weapon. Israel had nothing even remotely comparable in its arsenal—or so they supposed.

Like a walking oak tree, Goliath would lumber across to the Israelite battle line every day and bellow forth his challenge: "Why do you come out and line up for battle? Am I not a Philistine, and are you not the servants of Saul? Choose a man and have him come down to me. If he is able to fight and kill me, we will become your subjects; but if I overcome and kill him, you will become our subjects and serve us . . . . This day I defy the ranks of Israel! Give me a man and let us fight each other" (1 Sam. 17:8–10).

Needless to say, Saul felt a little pressured. As a matter of fact, Scripture says that "Saul and all the Israelites were *dismayed and terrified*" (1 Sam. 17:11).

Sometimes fear can be motivational. A football team with a healthy fear of their opponent will be encouraged to work out that much harder and hone their plays to perfection. But in Saul's case, paralysis had set in. Before the battle had even begun, he was already immobilized.

Who was the logical opponent to rise from Israel's ranks and face the colossal Philistine? *Saul* was. And he knew it. His office and experience made him the obvious choice. And beyond that, Saul stood a head taller than all of his countrymen (1 Sam. 9:2).

But Saul couldn't move. He had no options, no alternatives, and no plans whatsoever to cross swords with the giant. The next day it was the same story. Frozen, petrified. And again the next day. And the next. And the next. Saul and the armies of Israel endured Goliath's taunts "for forty days . . . every morning and evening"

(1 Sam. 17:16). That's nearly *six weeks* that the king of Israel sat terrified in his tent and did nothing!

In sailing terms, Saul was "in irons." He could move neither forward nor backward. Afraid to leave, afraid to stay, he was even more afraid to confront the problem head-on. With no inner motivation to change the status quo, Saul could only wait for the Philistines to take the initiative.

Pressure can have that same kind of effect on a 20th-century Christian as well. Sometimes life seems so demanding and complex. Like Saul, you see major challenges before you. Deep in your heart you know you should be making strides in your spiritual life; you know you need more schooling; you know you should be cultivating the friendship of your unsaved neighbors; you know you should sit down and rework your budget in a way that honors God. You know all those things. But it's difficult to move. Sometimes *agonizingly difficult*. Those disturbing "what if's" keep floating before your eyes.

"What if I fail again?"

"What if I'm ridiculed or rejected?"

"What if I don't have what it takes?"

"What if God doesn't come through for me?"

That's the real question, isn't it? You may call it "caution" or "prudence" or a "wait and see" attitude, when often the problem is simply unbelief.

Does God want you to grow, reach out, change, try, love, step out in faith for Him? Of course He does. Read through the prayers of Paul and note how the apostle is constantly praying that the believers scattered throughout the world would expand in their love, in their faith, in their giving, in their knowledge of God, in their sacrifice, in their service. Even a casual reading of the New Testament seems to shout out the message that "status quo" has no place in Christian thinking! How could it when every moment— every day— the believer is to be *conformed* to the image of God's Son?

When Saul confronted Goliath, the king's first reaction was a quick mental comparison of the giant's qualifications for battle with his own. Obviously, it was no contest. Saul's logic went something like this:

My training, weapons, strength, experience, size, courage and ability do not equal this man's training, weapons, strength, experience, size, courage and ability. Therefore, I am not equal to the challenge of Goliath.

Saul might have hid indefinitely behind his "logical" excuses for inactivity. But then one day a young shepherd boy came into camp with a sack full of bread and cheese for his soldier brothers, heard the Philistine's mocking words, and burned with indignation. *"Who is this uncircumcised Philistine that he should defy the armies of the living God?"* (1 Sam. 17:26).

David knew nothing of Saul's "logic." He had his own formula for sizing up a battle. Saul tried to straighten the boy out. "You are not able to go out against this Philistine and fight him; you are only a boy, and he has been a fighting man from his youth" (1 Sam. 17:33). But David would not be turned aside. "Your servant has killed both the lion and the bear," he told the king. "This uncircumcized Philistine will be like one of them because he has defied the armies of the living God. The Lord who delivered me from the paw of the lion and the paw of the bear will deliver me from the hand of this Philistine" (1 Sam. 17:36,37).

Saul then tried to persuade the young man to put on the king's own armor, but David would have none of it. When at last he faced the awesome Goliath in the valley he could cry out with conviction. "You come against me with sword and spear and javelin, but I come against you in the name of the Lord Almighty, the God of the armies of Israel, whom you have defied . . . All those gathered here will know that it is not by sword or spear that the Lord saves; for *the battle is the Lord's,* and he will give all of you into our hands" (1 Sam. 17:45,47).

David's logic looked like this:

My training, weapons, strength, experience, size, and ability do not equal his training, weapons, strength, experience, size, and ability. BUT MY GOD IS A MATCH FOR ANY GIANT. Therefore, in His strength, I am equal to any challenge He lays before me!

To whose logic do you subscribe? The logic of physical comparison and earthly reasoning . . . or the logic that says "We live by faith, not by sight . . . . I can do everything through him who gives me strength" (2 Cor. 5:7; Phil. 4:13)? Do the weights and worries of your daily life hold you hostage to pressure paralysis?

Why not practice David's formula? Your "Goliaths" may be different, but one part of the formula remains the same as it was 3,000 years ago: Your God is a match for any giant— any task— any situation. And He's eager to prove it to you and the whole watching world . . . if you'll just give Him the chance.

Pressure is a common denominator in the Christian life. As the strains and stresses grow and the weights pile on, you will find yourself seeking an outlet, an escape hatch, someplace to hide.

Saul tried to cope through frenzied activity ("Maybe I can run away from it") followed by paralyzed inactivity ("Maybe if I don't move it will go away"). If Saul would have only paused to seek a glimpse of life from God's perspective, he might have realized something significant about pressure. Saul's overwhelming circumstances were an open, loving invitation from God to discover the vast resources of heaven. Resources well able to equip the king for every situation. Leaving the invitation unopened, Saul missed a precious opportunity— in fact, the opportunity of a lifetime. But about then a shepherd boy came by and found the discarded invitation. Dusting it off, David claimed it for himself. From that time on, for years to come, there wasn't a giant in the land that could stand in David's way.

Make a mental list of the "giants" you are facing today. Now, take a quiet moment or two and remember that each difficult circumstance is a personal invitation from God to discover anew the grace He has waiting for you. Don't leave the invitation unopened. You might miss the opportunity of *your* lifetime.

Work It Through

1. When Saul was at Gilgal he listened to the "clamoring voice of circumstance" rather than the "still, small voice" of God's Holy Spirit. We all face that kind of decision in our daily lives. What are some practical ways we might train ourselves to hear *His* voice in the midst of our day-to-day pressures?

---

2. The account in 1 Samuel 13: 1–15 reveals that Saul had real problems with waiting for God's timing. Can you find any parallels with this situation in your own experience today? List several promises from God's Word that could help you to "wait on the Lord."

---

3. 1 Samuel 17 reveals Saul's crippling case of "pressure paralysis." David, however, when confronted with the very same threatening situation, took immediate, positive action. Compare and contrast Saul and David's evaluation of the Goliath situation.

---

4. This chapter called pressure in the Christian life a "loving invitation" from the Lord to walk closer with Him. Is this a realistic assessment? Why or why not? How has it proved true in your own experience?

NOTES

Introduction to

David

Amusement really isn't funny.

A close look at the word reveals some surprising things. "A-MUSE" means the absence of *musing*, or considering. When you are *amused* you are not thinking—or at least not thinking about anything important. When you go to an *amusement* park, you're entering a place where you won't have to consider—you won't have to think things through. When you turn on the TV for *amusement*, you're doing it so that you can set your mind in neutral. Another meaning of *amuse* involves diverting someone's attention so that you can deceive them.

Sometimes not thinking is nice. Even the brain needs a break now and then. But when amusement becomes a lifestyle, it isn't amusing—it's a tragedy. God created man to muse. He gave him the capacity to consider, to meditate. And if a man muses long enough, he might even muse about his Creator.

Augustine said, "Thou hast formed us for Thyself, and our hearts are restless until they find rest in Thee." In other words, there are deep longings in man's heart that only God can fill. That's why people can feel an unexplainable loneliness in the middle of a crowd, or even among family and friends. *Even a Christian can feel alone* if he or she has never discovered what it means to be God's companion.

Sometimes Christians talk about a relationship with Jesus Christ as though it were a formal business transaction. David understood it to be something more. The Old Testament shepherd-king unlocked doors of fellowship with God that very few people ever enter. That's surprising, because David left the keys within easy reach. The following pages describe several of those keys.

$\mathcal{D}avid's$ LIFE IN SUMMARY

The Shepherd
(1 Sam. 16:11; Ps. 23)

From early boyhood, David tends the flocks of Jesse his father. David's years of solitude in the barren hills and valleys of Judah do much to mold his character. During these lonely years David hones several skills. He becomes proficient at playing the harp; he composes numerous songs of worship and praise; he develops physical strength and endurance; and he becomes a confident marksman with a sling and stone. Most importantly, the young shepherd enjoys a deepening personal relationship with his God. Daring and courageous, David learns dependence on God as he fends off the wild beasts of the wilderness—a knowledge which will serve him well in later years as he struggles against even deadlier human foes.

The Fugitive
(1 Sam. 16-30)

After years of obscurity in the wilds of Judah, David finds himself suddenly thrust into the national limelight. First, the prophet Samuel visits Jesse's Bethlehem ranch and anoints David to succeed King Saul. Unaware of David's promotion, Saul summons David to become his court musician. When Goliath terrifies Israel's army, David fells the Philistine champion with a single stone. Saul, infuriated by jealousy over David's growing national acclaim, forces David to flee to the wilderness. For the next ten years, David lives the life of a fugitive. But willing to await God's timing, he is finally crowned King of Judah after Saul and his sons are slain in battle.

Focus	The Shepherd (1 Sam. 16:11; Ps. 23)		The Fugitive		
Divisions	David minds his father's sheep in the wilderness		Anointed by Samuel; appointed to Saul's court	Flees from Saul; builds an army of outlaws	Flees to the Philistines; victory over Amalekites
Topics	The Lord is my Shepherd		The Lord is my Shield		
	Solitude		Struggle		
	Responding to God		Running from Saul		
Place	Hill Country of Judah		Wilderness of Judah		
Approx. Dates (Age)	1040–1025 B.C. (Birth–15 yrs.)		1025–1011 B.C. (15–29 yrs.)		

The King in Triumph
(2 Sam. 1-10)

*F*ollowing Saul's death, David's fortunes soar. The "man after God's own heart" receives the kingship of Judah, and seven years later, sovereignty over all Israel. After establishing Jerusalem as his capital, David honors the Lord by returning the Ark of the Covenant to the center of Israel's national life. The Lord, in turn, honors David by giving him military victory on every hand. Zealous to promote God's name, David expresses a desire to construct a great temple to the Lord in the heart of Jerusalem. Although God denies the king his wish, He promises that one of David's own sons will build the temple, and that David's dynasty will never end!

The King in Crisis
(2 Sam. 11-24)

*S*torm clouds of shame, anguish, and violence darken the remaining years of David's life. The king's sorrows begin when he yields to the double sins of adultery and murder. Confronted by God's word through Nathan the prophet, David repents and is forgiven by the Lord. Consequences of David's sin, however, fill his remaining years with strife. Incest, murder, and rebellion tear at the king's family—and break the king's heart.

The cruelest blow of all comes when David's handsome and gifted son Absalom stages a coup, forcing his father into exile. Although Absalom is killed and David is restored to the throne, the king is consumed by grief for his son. The "sweet psalmist of Israel" dies a broken man at the age of 70.

The King in Triumph (2 Sam. 1-10)			The King in Crisis			
David's reign over Judah	David's reign over all Israel	David's kingdom expands	David's great sin and its consequences	Absalom's attempt to overthrow David	David's return to the throne	David's final days
The Lord is my Strength			The Lord is my Salvation			
Success			Sin and Sorrow			
Ruling Israel			Reaping Sin			
Hebron	Jerusalem		Jerusalem			
1011–990 B.C. (29–50 yrs.)			990–971 B.C. (50 yrs.–death)			

Companionship Developed

(Read: 1 Samuel 16)

With his flock bedded down for the night, the young shepherd draws a weathered cloak around his shoulders and lies back on the sparse grass of the hillside. A low wind whispers in the valley; a restless ewe bleats in the darkness.

And then there is silence. With eyes full of awe and wonder, the shepherd loses himself in the great sea of stars. Softly, reverently, a song breaks the stillness and rises into the night.

"O LORD, our Lord,

How majestic is your name in all the earth!

You have set your glory above the heavens."

These were nights the shepherd David would never forget. During those long hours of wilderness solitude, he fell in love with God. And God loved David, saying of him, "I have found David son of Jesse, a man after my own heart, who will do everything I want him to do" (Acts 13:22).

There were probably many in Israel who were faithful to God's commands. It is likely that thousands understood the teachings about Israel's one God, and observed the traditions and ceremonies handed down to them by their fathers and their fathers' fathers.

But David's life was different. In David's eyes, *God was a Companion.* Throughout those years on the sheep trails, David's God emerged from tradition and history to become a warm, personal Friend, one that David loved with all his heart, soul, mind and strength. As he led his flocks through the barren hills and pasture lands of Judah, David learned to relate everything in life—everything he saw, everything he felt—to that relationship with his Companion.

When he gazed up into the heavens at night, David did more than count stars; he marveled at the handiwork of a close Friend.

As he learned the ways of shepherding, he began to see *himself* as the sheep, needing the tender care of a Shepherd.

"Lord, You are *my* Shepherd. You give me everything I need. Sometimes I'm just like one of these foolish sheep. I wander away from You and get into all kinds of trouble. Then when I become lonely or afraid I cry out—and You're right there. There to heal my wounds. There to scoop me up in Your arms and put me back on the right trail."

When the storms came and David was forced to find refuge in a cave or in the shelter of some great rock, it made him think of the refuge he enjoyed in his God.

"Lord, You're just like this big rock to me. I can turn to You when I'm in trouble and You give me shelter and security. I can put my full confidence in You."

When David's path divided in front of him and he wasn't sure which way to turn, it reminded him that his Friend was always there to point the way.

"You have made known to me the path of life . . . . When my spirit grows faint within me, it is you who know my way" (Ps. 16:11; 142:3).

When David faced dangers in the wilderness, he simply placed his life in the hands of his Companion.

"Lord, that lion has one of my lambs—and I'm going to have to go after it. Thanks, Lord, that You're right beside me to deliver me from the mouth of that lion" (cf. 1 Sam. 17:34-36).

What a picture Scripture paints: David and God, the young shepherd and the Great Shepherd, walking together through life.

Have you ever found yourself dreaming about a lifestyle like that of young David's? Out in the wide open spaces somewhere. No charge account bills, no jangling telephones, no traffic signals, no alarm clocks. Just think of all the time you would have to meditate on God's creation and memorize portions of his Word. Seems like a person could really draw near to God in a situation like that, doesn't it? David had all the breaks!

But something strange appears when you look closer at David's family. Scripture says that David had seven older brothers. Brothers who grew up in the same home he did. Brothers who watched over Jesse's flocks just like he did. Brothers who wandered down the same paths, camped in the same places, went through the same training, learned from the same mother and father. But here is the strange part: *Not one of them* was a "man after God's own heart." Only David. God looked into the hearts of those seven brothers and found nothing to commend them.

But in 1 Samuel 16, when David walked before the prophet Samuel, God said, "That's the man. Pour the anointing oil on his head. David and I know each other well . . . we're friends" (cf 1 Sam. 16:1-13).

What was it that made the difference? It wasn't his location or occupation. It wasn't his family, his environment or his excess free time. What, then? What set him apart?

It was David's *heart*. A heart that refused to settle for a mediocre walk with God. A heart that rejected a lukewarm relationship. A heart that wanted the companionship of the Lord more than anything else in life.

It is easy to fall into a mindset that says, "If only I could change this or that about my life, I'd be a different man—a different woman. If only I could change some of my circumstances. If only some of the pressures and problems eased up a little. If only I could break free from this rat race and get into a different job and living situation, then I would have better fellowship with Jesus Christ."

When you look at the life of David it appears he had some unfair advantages because he grew up as a shepherd. Who has time for solitude and reflection these days? Who has time to stand for hours and gaze at the rustling grass or lie back and watch the stars? If only you were in David's sandals, you tell yourself, you could be more like him. You could enjoy the Lord the way he did.

All of this sounds plausible until you consider David's brothers Eliab, Abinadab, Shammah—they had quiet trails and starlit nights. They had time to meditate. But what became of them? After a brief entry in 1 Samuel 17, they disappear from the scene. You look for some record of their lives, and find only a blank record. Might that be an indication of how much their lives counted for the Lord?

And why might that be true? They had such marvelous circumstances and opportunities! They could have all been "men after God's own heart." But they were not, because they did not choose to be. They did not choose to make friendship with God a priority in their lives. They were not willing to pay the price that such a friendship involves. Other things in life were more important: their sheep, their homes, their careers in Saul's army, their reputations. If they had wanted closer fellowship with God, the opportunity was theirs to pursue. Because they did not really care, they never found that fellowship, and all the solitude and scenery in the world made little difference.

Would *you* be a different person if you could change your present set of circumstances? Would you love God more if you had a different job, a different home, a different schedule? Chances are you would not. Because wherever you go, whatever you do, you take your heart with you. And if your heart does not hunger for God right now, right where you are, it will not hunger for God somewhere else. If you find yourself drifting from fellowship with God, you do not need a change of scene. You need a change of heart.

The Lord called David to be a shepherd, and as a shepherd David used every opportunity to relate life to God. What has the Lord called you to do? Where has the Lord placed you? Are you making the most of every opportunity *right now* to reach out for God's companionship? Or do you find yourself so buried with cares and responsibilities and activities that God gets placed low in your list of priorities?

Life goes by so quickly, and the solemn fact is that you are either developing a life of companionship with God or you are rejecting it. You are either becoming a David or you are becoming like one of his brothers.

Do you sense deep inside that your life has become shallow . . . empty . . . estranged from the love of Jesus Christ? Then why not make today a day of real change in your life? *Make* time to get alone with God. *Make* time to read and study his Word. *Make* time to pour out your heart in prayer before him. It will never "just happen." With God's help, you can make it happen. By your own personal choice. By an act of your will. Let your friendship with God cut a wide swath down the middle of your life—touching everything you do, everything you are. Claim these words from Jeremiah as your very own:

" 'Then you will call upon me and come and pray to me, and I will listen to you. You will seek me and find me when you seek me with all your heart. I will be found by you,' declares the LORD" (Jeremiah 29:12-14).

Companionship Tested

(Read: 1 Samuel 21-31)

If anyone ever watched his fortunes rise and fall like a roller-coaster, it was David.

Psalm 78:70,71 says that God chose him and "took him from the sheep pens; from tending the sheep he brought him to be the shepherd of his people."

The psalmist mentions the fact that God *brought* David from the pasture to the palace. But he does not mention what God *brought him through* to get there. He does not mention the ten-year interval in between. Years of strife, fear, and loneliness. Years when David's companionship with God was severely tested.

At first, success came quickly for David. It all started with the secret anointing by Samuel. Things were never the same after that day. The quiet life of a shepherd, the tranquility of being a "nobody"— all of that was behind him forever.

Soon after the anointing, an unsuspecting King Saul put David on the royal payroll as court musician. God gave the teenager such favor in the king's eyes that Saul soon promoted him to the post of king's armor-bearer. Then came the showdown with Goliath. After that, there was no stopping David's rise to fame. Soon the former shepherd was leading a thousand men into battle, enjoying such phenomenal military success that all Israel was singing his praises. Scripture says, "In everything he did he had great success, because the LORD was with him" (1 Sam. 18:14).

But then the bottom dropped out. Trouble and heartache roared into David's life like a flood. In short order, he lost his job, was driven from his wife and home, was separated from his best friend, and was forced to flee to the wilderness for his very life. The same army he previously led in triumph only a few months earlier was now pursuing him as Public Enemy Number One.

For the next ten years of his life, David lived the life of a fugitive: constantly on the move; constantly in danger of capture and execution; running from one place to the next; hiding in lonely forests or lurking in limestone caves. *Ten years!* From about the age of 20 to the age of 30. Some of the choicest years of manhood. Years when a man normally establishes himself in a career and begins building his home and family. But for David, they were years of disappointment and struggle. One by one, he watched his dreams crumble into dust.

Now, what became of David's companionship with God? What happened to that "intimate friendship" between a man and his God? It is one thing to talk about fellowship with the Lord out in the hills or by the campfire at night. It is one thing to enjoy His presence when all the honors and accolades are rolling in. But it is something else to speak of friendship with God in a day of tragedy and hardship.

In David's case, that love bond became even stronger. If he loved God before, he *adored* Him now. If he leaned on the Lord's strength before, now he rested completely on Him. No longer could David rely on a secure home life. No longer could he depend on friends, popularity, personality, or skill. There was nothing left to hang onto but God, and David clung with all his might.

But why would God require David to experience those years of trouble at all? If He was truly David's Friend, why didn't He step in and put an end to it somehow?

Here are two possible reasons; one involves David, the other involves *you*.

In the first place, it may have been that David's friendship with God had reached a plateau—a leveling-off point. It is almost a truism that nothing in the spiritual life remains level. There is either an advance, or there is decline. If David was going to go on in his relationship with God, he had to experience God's grace in a deeper way. For that reason, in His love, the Lord allowed David to enter a period of pain and trial. No one really advances in his walk with God in a time of complete tranquility. No one develops muscles of faith and trust when everything is prosperity and peace. David's years as a fugitive brought him to the end of himself. And once he reached the limits of wisdom and endurance, David found resources beyond anything he had ever experienced. He began to tap the infinite resources of God, resources he would sorely need as the king of Israel!

The second possible reason for David's suffering cuts through the centuries to touch your life today. God gifted David with an ability to turn his soul inside-out. As no one before or since, David was able to record his innermost thoughts in both word and music. David wrote many of his *psalms* during those difficult years— songs which enable you to look into his heart, feel his anguish, and hear his whispered prayers. In the Psalms you can find hope and joy in the nearness of God, even though the world seems to be collapsing around you. Whatever your emotion, whatever your frame of mind, you can plunge into the Psalms and find a soul-mate. You can find your own personal struggles so clearly expressed, it often seems as if you're reading your own diary. You can find words and prayers that give expression to your deepest longings.

Something beautiful emerged from David's sorrow and pain. Those lonely years in the wilderness were not wasted. Not a single tear was shed in vain. The psalms that came forth from David's "crucible of crisis" have drawn believers closer to the God of heaven for nearly 3,000 years.

Take a minute to consider some of the pressures, disappoint-ments, and anxieties you have faced during the past few weeks. Perhaps right now you could name two or three areas of your life where you are hurting deeply or struggling privately.

Why is God allowing you to go through these hard times? Why doesn't He intervene right now and lift you out of those stressful situations? Could it be that your own walk with God has "leveled off"? Could it be that God wants to lift your friendship with Him to a whole new level?

Perhaps God wants to turn your life into a psalm. As you respond to Him in your stress, as you learn to pour out your heart in trusting prayer and find a new grasp on His sufficiency . . . there may be others who are watching. Others who have their own hurts, but don't know where to take them. Others who carry their own sorrows and know nothing of God's love and provision for their lives. As you reach out and find God's strong hand, others too may want to reach. Perhaps they too will find "the Father of Compassion and the God of all comfort" (2 Cor. 1:3).

What do people hear when they put their ears alongside your life today? Words of self-pity, or a song of trust?

A sigh . . . *or a psalm?*

Companionship Restored

(Read: 2 Samuel 11)

Real friendship is a hardy thing. It can survive blows and disappointments and come right back with new growth and fragrant blossoms. It can weather weeks of neglect, hanging on with the tenacity of an oak in a windstorm. But even the most firmly rooted friendship withers in the presence of deceit. Companionship can smile in the face of adversity, dig deeper and stand firm in a crisis, but it cannot live with a lie.

In one dark era of his life David embraced deceit and forfeited his most precious possession—the companionship of God. 2 Samuel 11 paints the picture in somber shades. David had become careless and lazy. One restless evening found him pacing the roof of his palace. He saw a beautiful woman bathing in a nearby house. He sent for her and, although he knew she was another man's wife, he slept with her. The woman, Bathsheba, became pregnant. David tried desperately to cover his involvement. When he couldn't, he had the woman's husband killed, and brought her into the palace as his own wife. Scripture says that "the thing David had done displeased the Lord" (2 Sam. 11:27).

David had sinned and knew it. But rather than face up to it, he chose to pretend there was nothing wrong. He kept busy. He ran the kingdom. He made appearances. He worshiped the Lord in a public, ceremonial way. He attended the right meetings, said the right words, and gave the right answers. Everything was right—except David's heart.

Deep down, he knew it was all deceit. He could not lift his face to the Companion of his youth. On certain sleepless nights the pain of his inner emptiness must have been almost unbearable. God's hand, once so welcome and reassuring, was now a dreaded thing, laying heavily on David's heart.

But then Nathan the prophet came to see the king. As God's spokesman, Nathan confronted the king with his sin. The prophet's pointed finger was all it took. David's defenses crumbled and he fell on his knees in confession and repentance. There was grief, there were bitter tears. But at last there was truth.

And what a difference it made! After the experience was behind him, David wrote, "Blessed (happy) is the man whose sin the Lord does not count against him *and in whose spirit is no deceit*" (Ps. 32:1,2). No deceit! No shadows, no clouds, no barriers to block communication with God. The backwash of David's sin would bring strife and heartache into his life for years to come, but David no longer had to bear it alone. He could take it to his Friend. He could share it with his Companion.

An incredible thing happened after David's confession.

God gave David a psalm. And then another and another. Sweet, clear music flowed from the harp that had been silent for so long. Psalms 32 and 51, written *after* David's sin and restoration to fellowship, have become beacons of hope for millions groping through the fog of sorrow and despair. God was able to use even the dark, painful chapter of David's life to bless others.

Warm, dynamic friendship with the living God cannot exist if there is unconfessed sin in your life. But once honest, open-hearted confession takes place, companionship *can* be restored. God *can* use you again. He can even use those days, weeks, or years seemingly wasted by sin and rebellion. How? by making your life into a psalm of His grace and love. When others see that you have found forgiveness, peace, and joy in the Lord, they may also be encouraged to seek His grace for *their* lives.

It all begins with an honest heart. Why not learn from "the man after God's own heart" and begin each new day with this prayer:
> "Search me, O God, and know my heart;
>   test me and know my anxious thoughts.
> See if there be any offensive way in me,
>   and lead me in the way everlasting" (Ps. 139:23,24).

Work It Through

1. David's brothers demonstrate that external circumstances do not necessarily determine one's walk with God. What then was the key spiritual difference between David and his older brothers?

_____

_____

_____

2. As a young man David experienced a drastic reversal in his fortunes: In a matter of weeks he went from being a national hero to a hated, hunted public enemy. For the next ten long years he endured the heart-breaking life of a fugitive. What are some possible reasons why God allowed the "man after His own heart" to go through these terrible trials?

_____

_____

_____

3. What is the meaning of the suggestion that God might wish to "turn your life into a psalm"?

_____

_____

_____

4. What does David mean in Psalm 32:2 when he writes about the happiness of having "no deceit" in one's spirit? Draw parallels between this verse and the prayer in Psalm 139:23,24.

_____

_____

_____

NOTES

Solomon

The year is 970 B.C., and you are faced with one of the most difficult challenges of your long, infamous career. *How are you going to trap the wisest man who has ever lived?* His name is Solomon. He's the son of David, one of your archenemies. And the Lord has equipped him with wisdom and discernment beyond that of any man who has ever walked the earth. To make matters infinitely worse, Solomon loves the Lord . . . the Lord whom you despise.

What a predicament! How do you corner a man like that? How do you trip up a man with the resources of Solomon? It seems almost hopeless. If you were anyone else, you might be tempted to give up and find more vulnerable targets. But because you are who you are, you will not give up. *You* will be patient. *You* will bide your time and wait for an opening. It's that important to you. Because you know that if you can outwit the wisest man in the world, you can outwit anyone. If you can develop a strategy to ruin Solomon's life, you will be able to employ it for generations to come on millions of God's people.

And that would give you great delight . . . if your name was Satan.

Unless otherwise indicated, Scripture quotations in this chapter are from the New American Standard Bible.

Solomon's LIFE IN SUMMARY

Solomon the Prince
(2 Sam. 12-18)

As if God were showing that He could bring good out of even a terrible situation, the union of David and Bathsheba results in the birth of Solomon. The couple's first child was stricken by God and died as a result of David's great sin, but the life of this second child shows great promise even while he is an infant. Nathan, the prophet who confronted David with his sin, now brings a message of encouragement: The child is deeply loved by the Lord and "for the Lord's sake," he is given the special name of Jedediah (loved of the Lord) in addition to his given name.

Solomon's Early Reign
(1 Kings 1-3)

By the time Solomon reaches the age of 20, his father David's life is drawing to a close. Adonijah, oldest son of David, makes a major attempt to claim the throne even though Solomon is the rightful heir. In one of his last public acts, David proclaims Solomon as his successor. Once in command, the young king quickly consolidates his power by eliminating several bitter enemies. God also confirms Solomon's rule by offering him whatever he desires. Solomon's choice of wisdom to rule justly pleases the Lord and the king is given wealth and honor as well.

Focus	Solomon the Prince (2 Samuel 12–18)			Solomon's Early Reign (1 Kings 1–3)		
Divisions	Conceived after death of David & Bathsheba's first child	Born to David & Bathsheba, loved by the Lord	Raised in the palace amid great family turmoil	Elevated to the throne after Adonijah's unsuccessful coup	Consolidating power, eliminating enemies	God's offer, Solomon's choice of Wisdom
Topics	Promise of Power			Possession of Power		
	Loved by the Lord			Loved the Lord		
	Learning Wisdom			Requesting Wisdom		
Place	Jerusalem			Jerusalem		
Approx. Dates (Age)	990–970 B.C. (Birth–20 yrs.)			970–966 B.C. (20–24 yrs.)		

Solomon's Golden Years
(1 Kings 4-10)

With his throne secure and his land at peace, Solomon begins work on the greatest project of his life: construction of a magnificent temple for the Lord's dwelling place. With cedar from Lebanon, huge stones from mountain quarries, and an army of laborers from all over Israel, Solomon oversees the project that will take seven years to complete. God shows His love and favor to Israel by filling the new temple with His glory as Solomon leads the people in a heartfelt prayer of dedication. As the years go by, Solomon grows mighty in wealth, wisdom and power.

Solomon's Sad Decline
(1 Kings 11)

Busy with building projects and the accumulation of wealth, Solomon finds little time for the Lord. Throughout his life, Solomon had ignored God's command against intermarrying with pagan women. Now, in his middle years, the sin begins to bear bitter fruit in his life. The 700 wives and 300 concubines of his royal harem draw his heart away from Israel's God, introducing him to the worship of foreign gods and idols. Angry at Solomon's apostasy, the Lord reveals that He will tear the kingdom from the hand of Solomon's son.

Solomon's Golden Years (1 Kings 4–10)				Solomon's Sad Decline (1 Kings 11)		
Building the temple	Building the palace	Dedicating the temple	Fortifying the country	Solomon's wives and idolatry	Solomon's adversaries	Solomon's death
Peak of Power				Passing of Power		
Built for the Lord				Turned from the Lord		
Living Wisely				Living Foolishly		
Jerusalem				Jerusalem		
966–950 B.C. (24–40 yrs.)				950–931 B.C. (40 yrs.–Death)		

Solomon and Satan's Secret Weapon

(Read: 1 Kings 11)

How would you do it if you were Satan? How would you draw a person away from his love for God and his desire to serve Him?

Whatever your tactics, you know that defeating Solomon will be an uphill battle—all the way.

Even while Solomon was still an infant God expressed a special love for him. 2 Samuel 12:24,25 records how the Lord sent Nathan the prophet to David and Bathsheba with a message about their child. Through Nathan, God gave David's son the sacred name *Jedediah*—"loved by the Lord."

And Solomon responded to that divine love as he matured. Under the influence of godly parents and the watchful eye of Nathan, the prince grew up with a heart for God. In Proverbs 4, Solomon recalls the long talks he had with his father, David. As they walked together in the royal gardens or looked out into the distance from the wall of the city, "the man after God's own heart" must have urged his son to develop a deepening relationship with the Lord.

Nathan the prophet would have remembered clearly the Lord's tender love toward Prince Solomon, and undoubtedly reminded the boy many times of his special destiny.

Little wonder that as Solomon ascended to the throne of Israel he "loved the Lord, walking in the statutes of his father David" (1 Kings 3:3).

His reign began like a spring sunrise, full of life and hope and promise. It was a fresh breeze blowing across Israel, and it had about it the fragrance of peace and great things to come.

What a beginning! If ever a king pointed his people toward the worship of God, it was Solomon. He poured the strength of his youth and all his vast creative energies into the building of an awesome temple for the honor of the Lord's name. At the time of the temple's dedication, he got down on his knees before the whole nation and cried out to God on behalf of his people. How zealous he was to serve Him!

So there you are. As the adversary of God, you have a real problem on your hands. How do you topple that kind of bedrock commitment? How do you cast a shadow across a life so radiant with faith and love for God?

You might think back on all your other victories . . . thumb through your "Favorite Strategy" file . . . and remember how you had ruined the lives of so many of God's people down through the years. But will these well-worn techniques work on a Solomon?

Well, how did you approach Solomon's father? Let's see now, where is that "David" file? There's Dan, Daniel (now *there* was a wasted effort!), Darius, Dathan—ah, *David*. How could you forget? David was crippled by a direct frontal assault. One withering blast of temptation at a moment of weakness was enough to sweep him off his feet. *Very* satisfying indeed. But Solomon . . . Solomon is much too wise for that.

Your eye catches the "Eve" file. One of your all-time favorite files. What a triumph! And all it took were a few well-placed questions to open a wedge of doubt in her heart. Simple, very simple. But oh, so effective down through the years. But Solomon? He has much too much discernment to be jolted by a line like that.

No doubt about it, Solomon presents a tactical situation that requires all the sophistication and subtlety you can muster. For a job like this, you'll have to make use of a special weapon. From the depths of your darkest closet, you bring out that strategy you've been saving a thousand years for just such an occasion. Carefully you unwrap it . . . turn it lovingly in your hands . . . and admire its subtle beauty.

What was Satan's secret weapon? Really, it was so simple. All the Adversary had to do was to get Solomon *preoccupied*. And that is where the cunning ingenuity of Satan's scheme emerges. Because the first thing the devil did was to get Solomon busy in the Lord's work! Building the temple!

Now it had been in God's plans for Solomon to build a temple. And the structure he raised to the skies in Jerusalem was astonishingly beautiful—one of the architectural marvels of the ancient world. Trouble was, Solomon never found much time to worship in the temple. He was too busy, too preoccupied with all the additional building projects he had begun. Just building a temple wasn't enough. He had the "building fever" now and he couldn't put down all the new plans and blueprints.

In Ecclesiastes, Solomon describes several of the projects he began after completing the temple:

"I enlarged my works: I built houses for myself, I planted vineyards for myself; I made gardens and parks for myself, and I planted in them all kinds of fruit trees; I made ponds of water for myself to irrigate a forest of growing trees" (Eccl. 2:4-6).

Building the Lord's temple had taken seven years. The construction of Solomon's own personal palace took *thirteen*.

Perhaps when Solomon was in the midst of constructing the temple he sensed that his own personal walk with the Lord was not what it had been. "But," he could have reasoned, "this is the Lord's work. As soon as I'm finished here, there will be time to seek God's face as my father sought him." When the temple was completed, however, there were other concerns.

"Where am I going to house this Egyptian princess I've married? What if Pharaoh came up to visit his daughter and found her living in this old palace of my father's? Of course it isn't a *bad* place. Dad put a lot of work into it . . . but it doesn't really have much *class*. I'll build a place that will do credit to the city where the Lord lives. I'll please the Lord by making this city the showplace of the world! Then, when I really get this place shaped up, I'll devote my time to seeking the Lord like David my father did."

So the building went on and on. Project after project. Year after year. Saws and hammers echoed throughout the city and Solomon could be found at each construction site, his great, creative mind deeply involved in each aspect, each detail.

All too soon, however, Solomon found himself a tired old man. Looking out over everything he had built—all the marvelous buildings, parks, and projects—he could only shake his head sadly and say, "It was all emptiness. Wasted time. Like chasing the wind." The years were gone and his heart was far from the Lord. He had not followed in the footsteps of his father; he had not lived up to the tender name God had given him while he was still in the arms of his mother: "*Jedediah*—loved of the Lord." If he still remembered the name at all, it must have been a prick to his conscience. He had done so little to respond to that special divine love.

Preoccupation! What a master stroke by Satan! The secret weapon worked like a slow poison, gradually diverting and distracting Solomon's eyes from the Lord, gradually chilling his love for God and his zeal to serve Him. By the time Solomon realized what had happened to his life, it was already too late. He was an old man, life was behind him, opportunities were behind him and all he could do was pen his bitter regrets.

The "preoccupation weapon" worked so well for Satan—even on the wisest man in the world—that he has continued to employ it down through the centuries on God's people.

Centuries after Solomon, Jesus Christ wrote to a group of Christians in Laodicea. Like Solomon, they had become preoccupied with pride and wealth. Although they were born-again individuals, Jesus was outside of their affections, outside the door of their hearts. And it was to these Christians that the Son of God wrote: "Here I am! I stand at the door and knock. If anyone hears My voice and opens the door, I will go in and eat with him and he with Me" (Rev. 3:20 NIV).

Jesus *had* to knock. How else do you get someone's attention when they're preoccupied?

Christians have to be on constant alert or they may become as distracted and preoccupied by the world as a TV "addict" is preoccupied by the screen before his eyes. His wife may address him in pleading tones, his kids may dismantle the room around him, the dog and cat may engage in mortal combat inches from his feet. But the viewer is oblivious to all these things. They are like sounds from another world. The world you live in can be like a narcotic if you're not on guard against Satan's schemes. The apostle John wrote:

> "Never give your hearts to this world or to any of the things in it. A man cannot love the Father and love the world at the same time. For the whole world-system, based as it is on men's primitive desires, their greedy ambitions and the glamour of all that they think splendid, is not derived from the Father at all, but from the world itself" (1 John 2:15,16 Phillips).

Even God's work can become a dangerous preoccupation if it continually distracts you from seeking God's daily presence. Satan's secret weapon is so subtle.

Could it be that Jesus Christ has been knocking on the door of your heart during the last few weeks? How would He seek to gain your attention if you were preoccupied? Would He have to send trials . . . pain . . . overwhelming circumstances? Or would a restless heart and a lack of deep inner peace tell you that the Lord of your heart is knocking, seeking admission to the center of your love and affection?

Can you hear Him knocking right now? Why not find a quiet place and check the front door of your heart. He'll still be there, just like He's been there all along. God's love is very patient.

The Weeds in Solomon's Garden

(Read: Deuteronomy 17: 14-20)

Solomon never needed any encouragement to pull his royal chariot off to the side of the road. When you are the wisest man in the world, you're interested in almost everything. Bees, flowers, trees, lizards, ants—you name it. It was a wonder the king ever got anywhere, there were so many interesting things to see and investigate.

So when Solomon ordered the royal entourage to halt along a country road one afternoon, his attendants merely exchanged glances and did as they were told. What the king of Israel could *possibly* find to interest him along this forsaken stretch of highway defied the imagination.

Climbing out of the chariot, the king walked thoughtfully through the tall weeds at the edge of the roadway and stared out across a field and vineyard (neither of which seemed worthy of royal attention). The horses were beginning to paw the ground with impatience before Solomon turned and walked back to the company.

"Hmmm," he said. And that was all. The little band resumed its journey to Jerusalem and the palace.

But late that night as the king reclined on his couch and stared into the embers of a dying fire, he thought again about the farm he had seen by the side of the road. Taking up scroll and quill, the son of David penned these words:

I passed by the field of the sluggard,
And by the vineyard of the man lacking sense;
And behold, it was completely overgrown with thistles,
Its surface was covered with nettles,
And its stone wall was broken down.
When I saw, I reflected upon it;
I looked and received instruction.
"A little sleep, a little slumber,
A little folding of the hands to rest,"
Then your poverty will come as a robber,
And your want like an armed man (Prov. 24:30-33).

Little did the king know that he was writing a prophecy of himself. The characteristics of the sluggard's farm became the characteristics of Solomon's heart. By the time he had reached his middle years, many of Solomon's cherished values were broken down. The fine speeches and prayers of his early years were like so much chaff, strewn on a sluggard's field. Worthless thistles and stinging nettles grew thick in the very center of his life.

It all started with just a few small, hardly noticeable weeds. His marriage to the daughter of Pharaoh, for example. That kind of matrimonial arrangement was common in Solomon's day. One king would make an alliance with another king and to seal the arrangement would give his daughter as a bride. That made the kings in-laws, and who wants to go to war with your in-laws?

So Solomon sealed a deal with Pharaoh and brought the Egyptian princess into the house of David as his queen. Nothing unusual; nothing out of the ordinary. There was only one problem: It violated God's commands. Israelites were not to intermarry with pagan people, so that they would not become ensnared by the worship of foreign gods.

In fact, that is exactly what happened to Solomon. In 1 Kings 11:1-8, God lists the daughter of Pharaoh as one of the foreign women who finally turned Solomon's heart away from God. Jerusalem's society columns may have called the ceremony a glittering, gala affair; Israel's state department may have called it a stroke of political genius. But God called it sin. The marriage was a weed in Solomon's life. A little weed that would become a treacherous, life-sapping vine.

There were other weeds. Like the weed of wealth. According to Deuteronomy 17:17, a king on the throne of Israel was not to accumulate large hordes of silver and gold. But Solomon did just that. Another weed poked up its ugly head in the soil of Solomon's garden.

An Israelite king was not to "multiply wives for himself, lest his heart turn away" (Deut. 17:17). Solomon had 700 wives, and 300 concubines. And his heart *did* turn away.

The same passage in Scripture states that the king should not become a keeper of horses. Solomon ignored God's Word and incorporated 1,400 chariots and 12,000 horsemen into his army. The weeds grew thicker and thicker, slowly blocking out the light.

God had said that the king of Israel was not to rule in such a way that his head would become lifted in pride over his countrymen (Deut. 17:20). But Solomon fashioned for himself a gigantic throne of gold and ivory, adorned with 12 carved lions on its ascending steps. The Bible says that "nothing like it was made for any other kingdom." How distant and imposing and god-like Solomon must have looked seated on his great throne, robed in all his glory (Matt. 6:28,29). How far above the common folk of Israel who worked in the fields and paid their taxes! But it was not as God intended. Solomon's pomp and pride were poisonous plants in his garden.

Funny thing about weeds. They have a stubborn streak built into their very essence. Weeds are as old as sin. They began plaguing man the moment he rebelled against his Creator and was turned out of the Garden of Eden. No matter where they grow in all the world, it's always the same: Once they've taken root, they want to take over. A humble dandelion can push its head through a stone wall. In a matter of weeks, an unattended garden can be completely overgrown.

That was Solomon's problem. Like the sluggard in his own proverb, Solomon let down his guard. He became spiritually careless and lazy. Busy running the affairs of an empire, he neglected the affairs of his own soul. He took his relationship with God for granted and let the little weeds grow into big ones. Before long, sprawling vines, unsightly thorns and stinging nettles choked out the once-luscious fruit and strangled his love for God.

Ecclesiastes, written in his later years, is the testimony of a bitter, defeated man. It is the sad reminiscing of a man looking out over the grotesque remains of what was once a lovely, promising garden.

How does a Christian keep the garden of his or her soul free from weeds? How do you keep the harmful seeds from drifting over the wall of your life? Answer: *You can't*. Christians live in a weed-infested world. You are surrounded every day by godless philosophies, impure language and all kinds of degrading, suggestive input from the media.

What potential for a weedpatch! You can't keep weeds from coming in. *But you can keep weeds from taking over.* You can grab a hoe, roll up your sleeves and go to work in that garden of yours. How often should you work at weeding? It all depends on how deeply you want the weeds to become rooted in your soul. The more firmly they become entrenched, the harder they are to pull.

Solomon was right when he said, "A little sleep, a little slumber, a little folding of the hands to rest, then your poverty will come as a robber, and your want as an armed man." In other words, it doesn't take much to ruin a garden. It doesn't take much apathy or carelessness or prayerlessness to destroy potential fruit. Only "a little sleep." Only "a little folding of the hands." And suddenly you wake up to your poverty. Suddenly you realize what a barren, fruitless life you've been living. Suddenly you wonder what happened to your potential and where all the years have gone.

Did you meet the Lord at the gate of your inner garden this morning? You'll never find a better, more loving Gardener. You can trust Him to distinguish the weeds from the flowers in your life— the worthy from the worthless. You can trust him to handle the sharp sword of his Word with both firmness and gentleness as He uproots hurtful attitudes and prunes away life-sapping preoccupations. He can catch those destructive weeds while the roots are still young and shallow. Or, if He has to, He can clean out a garden that's been overgrown for years.

The Lord's weeding process may be painful. But you can be assured of one thing: The garden that's under the control of the Master Gardener will not fail to produce fruit.

Work It Through

1. Even though Solomon had never asked for it, God gave him great wealth (1 Kings 3:5-15). How could Solomon have avoided letting it become such a stumbling block to him?

_____

_____

2. Solomon had great wisdom and discernment from the Lord— more than any other man. Yet he failed so tragically and fell into sin. How could a man with so much knowledge of God end up so far away from Him? What characteristics must accompany wisdom and knowledge in your life if you are to have a growing walk with Christ?

_____

_____

3. Is it possible for a Christian to become preoccupied with "things" and never realize it? What are three practical ways you can guard against preoccupation in your life that excludes the Lord?

_____

_____

4. What are the two "thorns" that Jesus identifies in Matt. 13:3-23? Try to identify the two major thorns (or "weeds") in your own life that keep you from being more fruitful in your Christian life.

_____

_____

5. Hebrews 12:15 speaks about a "root of bitterness" springing up in someone's life. What does the verse say the results will be if the root is allowed to go on growing? Since Scripture refers to bitterness as a root, what characteristics of roots come to your mind? What makes deeply-rooted sins in your life so hard to deal with?

_____

_____

NOTES

Elisha

Elisha

It was hot, exhausting work. Not that burying a man's body was supposed to be joyful, but the close proximity of fierce Moabite raiding parties made the task doubly dismal. The small band of Israelites kept nervously glancing over their shoulders as they climbed the rocky incline toward the new tomb. The weight of the carefully wrapped body seemed to increase with each step.

Maintaining a respectful silence, they passed by the tomb of Elisha, the great prophet who in his long life had done so much for the people of Israel and—*what was that*? Hoofbeats! Horses! Wild Moabite war whoops! Shelter. They had to seek shelter in the rocks. But what about the body? They couldn't just leave it in the trail. Ah! Elisha's grave. They would hide the body in the prophet's tomb. Quickly, two of them put their shoulders to the stone that sealed the tomb's entrance. Two more tossed the body into the dark opening. Then they all crouched low.

Not one of them looked back at the tomb. Not one of them noticed that something was emerging. Perhaps it was the sound of heavy breathing that made them turn. Or perhaps it was a muffled cry. Suddenly the issue of Moabite raiders seemed unimportant. The body they had carried up the mountain was now staggering toward them, tearing at its graveclothes. Very much alive.

Could it be? Could it be that the prophet so full of God's kindness and power could perform such a miracle even after his death? How bizarre! And yet—how fitting. It was really the crowning touch on a life so yielded to God that its influence would reach down through the centuries. It can even reach to you. The unforgettable lessons of Elisha's life bestow life on any who consider the timeless truths woven through his unique ministry.

Elisha, the Farmer's Son
(1 Kings 19:15-20)

*I*n a nation wracked by political and religious turmoil, the farm of Shaphat provides a loving, godly island of peace and tranquility. Elisha, the son of Shaphat, grows up into a kind, sensitive young man, with an evident love for Jehovah, the God of Israel. By contrast, wicked King Ahab and Queen Jezebel are leading the Israelites farther and farther from the Lord. Idols of Baal and Ashteroth begin to dot the landscape. At the same time, stories are circulating of a fiery prophet named Elijah who is continually confronting Ahab and Jezebel. The word comes back that this spokesman for the Lord is endowed with incredible powers and is both feared and hated by the cation's rulers.

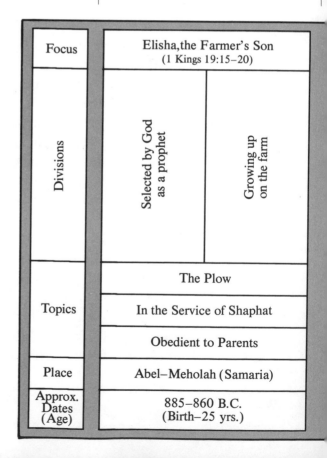

Focus	Elisha, the Farmer's Son (1 Kings 19:15–20)	
Divisions	Selected by God as a prophet	Growing up on the farm
Topics	The Plow	
	In the Service of Shaphat	
	Obedient to Parents	
Place	Abel–Meholah (Samaria)	
Approx. Dates (Age)	885–860 B.C. (Birth–25 yrs.)	

Elisha, the Follower
(1 Kings 19:19-2 Kings 2:12)

*U*nsettling national news must have sounded a little far away to Elisha on the farm in Abel-Meholah. The household of Shaphat was probably more concerned about the effects of the three and a half year drought. But once the drought is broken and the soil is moist and productive again, Shaphat sends Elisha and 11 others out to the fields, each with his own team of oxen. As Elisha plows, he notes the approach of Elijah. The prophet throws his mantle over the shoulders of Elisha, indicating God's choice of the young man to succeed Elijah as prophet. Sensing God's call, Elisha bids his family farewell and begins his 10-year ministry of encouragement and service to Elijah the Tishbite.

Elisha, the Faithful Prophet
(2 Kings 2:13-13:21)

*E*lisha's life reaches a crisis point as he realizes Elijah will soon be taken into heaven. Not only will Elisha be torn away from his master and companion, but he must consider the sobering responsibility of following as Elijah's successor. As the final moments of Elijah's earthly life tick away, he turns to his young aide with a question: "What can I do for you before I'm taken from you?" Aware of his needs and the uncertain road ahead, Elisha asks for and is granted a double portion of his master's spirit. The realization of that request is confirmed time and again during Elisha's long and miraculous career, as he performs fully twice as many miracles as his predecessor.

Elisha, the Follower (1 Kings 19:19–2 Kings 2:12)		Elisha, the Faithful Prophet (2 Kings 2:13–13:21)		
Commissioned by Elijah	Companion to Elijah	Established as God's prophet	A ministry of miracles in Israel	Elisha's final prophecy
The Towel		The Mantle		
In the shadow of the prophet		In the spirit of Elijah		
Obedient to Elijah		Obedient to God		
Throughout Samaria		Throughout Samaria		
860–850 B.C. (25–35 yrs.)		850–800 B.C. (35–85 yrs.)		

The Man in the Shadow
(Read: 1 Kings 19)

Elijah and Elisha.

Have you ever gotten their names mixed up? If someone asked you—right now—to draw a distinction between their two separate careers, could you do it? If not, don't be too hard on yourself. Their names sound so much alike and their lives are so closely associated with one another that very few people can separate the two.

Nevertheless, they *were* different men. Very different. Each man had his own unique story; each life has its own distinct message for today's believer.

Elisha was one of those persons who lived much of his life in the shadow of a great individual. In more ways than one, Elijah came first, followed by Elisha. Elijah blazed the trails, Elisha enlarged them. Elijah was the prophet of fire—a wild, fierce-looking individual who lived in the wilderness and clothed himself with the skins of wild animals. Elisha's ministry was less dramatic. He was the son of a well-to-do farmer, enjoyed living in cities, and relished the comforts of home.

Throughout most of his life, Elisha's ministry was eclipsed by the awesome reputation of his predecessor. Even after Elijah was gone from the scene and Elisha was well-established in his own work, he was still known as the man who "used to pour water on the hands of Elijah" (2 Kings 3:11).

Even today, it's much the same. Christian bookstores stock a number of recent studies on the life of Elijah. Ministers across the country draw sermon material from the dramatic biblical accounts of the Tishbite's prophetic ministry. For generations, a special chair has been set for Elijah at the circumcision ceremonies of every Jewish boy.

And Elisha? He remains in the shadows . . . the obscure understudy of a great prophet.

Somehow, I don't think Elisha would be troubled at this lack of recognition. *Even though God performed twice as many miracles through Elisha as He did through Elijah*, the former would probably be content to be remembered as the man who followed Elijah.

The story of Elisha begins as Elijah's public ministry is drawing to a close. The first mention of his name occurs in 1 Kings 19:16, as the Lord is counseling a bone-weary, thoroughly discouraged Elijah.

In a dramatic showdown with Ahab and the prophets of Baal, Elijah exposed the impotence of Baal worship in front of all Israel. In response to Elijah's prayer, a torrent of fire fell from heaven to consume a sacrifice and altar that had been drenched with water. As the rebellious people of Israel fell prostrate before the power of the Lord, Elijah had all 450 of the false prophets of Baal seized and executed in the Kishon valley.

Accomplishing this, he again sought the Lord's face in prayer and announced that a great rainstorm would break Samaria's three-and-a-half-year drought—even though there wasn't a cloud in the sky at the time. As the promised rain surged through Israel's sun-hardened gulleys, Elijah ran the 25 miles from Mt. Carmel to Jezreel. But upon hearing that Israel's evil queen Jezebel was out to kill him, the prophet ran an additional 100-mile marathon into the wilderness of Judah. Exhausted and depressed, he crawled under a desert broom-tree and called upon God to take his life.

At this point, Elisha's name enters the account. God moved in to minister to his weary servant with food, rest and encouragement. God directed Elijah to anoint Elisha as his successor in the ministry.

It was important that Elijah find an heir-apparent to carry on his important work. God knew that. But He also knew something else. He knew that Elijah needed a friend. He needed a companion to share the triumphs and defeats, the moments of joy and the moments of despair.

Elisha's first ministry was simply to become Elijah's friend. To be a listening ear; to offer words of counsel. To just be there. It was true that Elisha poured water over Elijah's hands as a servant. But more important than that, he poured the refreshing water of encouragement over Elijah's heart as a close companion. For ten years, until the older prophet was finally called into the presence of the Lord, Elisha served Elijah, walked the dusty roads of Samaria with him, and stood by his side until the very end.

It's easy to overlook a ministry of friendship and encouragement. Often it goes unnoticed. It isn't the kind of ministry that grabs a lot of attention and headlines. Jonathan was David's friend at a critical time in David's life. David went on to the throne and to fame and renown, but it was Jonathan who had stood beside him. It was Jonathan who had encouraged the son of Jesse when David felt like life wasn't worth living.

Paul initiated the major first-century thrust for Christian missions, but as you read his letters you discover it was several supportive friends who made the difference in his life: a Barnabas . . . an Onesiphorus . . . a Timothy.

Has God called you to a "background" ministry of encouragement? Has He gifted you by His Spirit with the abiity to come alongside another and strengthen his or her hand? Don't despise that gift. Don't allow yourself to feel that yours is a lesser calling. You may never bask in the sunlight of great acclaim. You may never enjoy the fame and renown of a dynamic, aggressive personality like an Elijah, a David or a Paul. But for a Christian, the bottom line of ministry has nothing whatsoever to do with the acclaim and recognition of men. The real evaluation takes place when the Lord Christ tallies up your life. And when that happens, many that are last will be first. Many that are in "starring roles" now will have to step back in wonder at a man or woman emerging from the shadows of obscurity—to receive the acclaim of heaven.

The Man and the Mantle

(Read: 2 Kings 2:1-15)

Fiction writers could never hope to duplicate the astonishing real-life drama portrayed in 2 Kings chapter 2.

The time has come for Elijah to be taken from the earth. His work is over. Before the day is through, God will send for him and Elisha will be left alone to carry on the work.

Elijah knows that. So does Elisha.

What if you knew for a fact that today was your last day on earth? What would you do? Where would you go? With whom would you want to spend your last few hours?

Elijah felt compelled in his spirit to visit the cities where he had established (or maintained) schools of prophets. He wanted his last views of Planet Earth to include the reassurance that the work of prophecy in Israel would be carried forward. He wanted to leave with the conviction in his heart that God's name would continue to be lifted up among His rebellious people.

"I'm going on my own," he told Elisha. "The Lord is sending me to Bethel. You stay here."

Elisha replied "As surely as the Lord lives and as you live, I will not leave you" (2 Kings 2:2).

The air must have held a strange tension as the pair walked from Gilgal to Bethel. There was that certain ominous feeling that something was going to happen—at any moment. A whirlwind was coming. A whirlwind that would wrench apart a friendship. Perhaps it would come as they rounded the next corner or descended the next hill. Elijah and Elisha were silent as they walked. Both men sensed the hush before a storm. It was coming and neither man could stop it.

As they arrived in Bethel at the school of the prophets, a small band of men was gathered outside the door. Elijah gazed upon the men who would prophesy to Israel in the Lord's name. He took time to search each face. Perhaps something in Elijah's eyes— something awesome, something almost unearthly—kept the men from speaking to their leader. They could only look on him, knowing what was to come. Turning instead to Elisha they said:

"Do you know that the Lord is going to take your master from you today?"

"Yes, I know," Elisha replied, "but do not speak of it" (2 Kings 2:3).

There it was. The affirmation of the inevitable. Repeated like the solemn tolling of a distant bell.

Again Elijah asked his servant to remain where he was, and again Elisha refused. Could the younger man simply stand and watch as his beloved teacher and closest companion walked off into the distance and disappeared over the horizon? He could not; he would not. Let the whirlwind come, but only the hand of God would separate Elisha from his master and friend.

As they arrived in Jericho, they were met by the company of prophets in that city. Again Elisha was warned of what he already knew. Again he walked on by Elijah's side.

Fifty of the prophets stood and watched at a distance as Elijah and Elisha approached the Jordan River. As their feet touched the bank, Elijah struck the surface of the water with his cloak and the water responded by opening a pathway before them. As they crossed over and stepped on the opposite bank, Elijah turned to regard his friend. What an encouragement the face of Elisha must have been to the old prophet as he drew so near to his departure. It's easy to imagine Elijah smiling in spite of himself and clasping his partner's shoulder. This successor of his was cut from stubborn material! Not even the rushing waters of the Jordan could come between them. It would take a wider, darker river than that to turn away a man with such love and determination.

Perhaps the sky began to darken as Elijah faced his companion. Perhaps the wind began to blow through the old man's gray hair and beard as their eyes locked in a final embrace.

"Tell me," the prophet said. "What can I do for you before I am taken from you?"

The answer came without hesitation. "Let me inherit a double portion of your spirit," Elisha replied. (2 Kings 2:9)

What Elisha was asking for was the blessing of a father for his oldest son. In those days, the oldest son would inherit a double portion of his father's wealth and blessing at the time of his father's death. Elisha had left his own father, land, and inheritance years before to follow the lonely prophet. Elijah was the only family he had. So Elisha asked him for the blessing a departing father would bequeath to his son and heir.

But what did Elijah own? What did he have to give? He had no land, no servants, no livestock or money. All that he possessed was his calling as a prophet and the worn skin cloak that had kept him warm through the long nights in the wilderness. These were Elijah's possessions. But for Elisha, it was enough.

By asking the question he did, the younger man was saying, "My father, if you must leave me, then leave me something of yourself. I'm not the man you are; I do not possess the strength you possess. And yet God is calling me to step into your place. How can I do that? How can I minister, my father, unless you grant me a double portion of your spirit, of your strength, of your zeal for the name of the Lord?"

"You have asked a difficult thing," Elijah said, "yet if you see me when I am taken from you, it will be yours—otherwise not" (2 Kings 2:10).

Then as they walked on, still deep in conversation, Elijah's moment came. The whirlwind descended, and Elisha caught a glimpse of flaming horses and a chariot of fire. In a matter of moments, he was alone. As he faced the Jordan once more, Elisha took his master's cloak, crying out, "Where now is the Lord, the God of Elijah?" (2 Kings 2:14) and struck the water.

Instantly, the river obeyed. The double portion was his.

Perhaps today you find yourself in a situation similar to that of Elisha. You are faced with demands and responsibilities that sometimes seem like more than you can bear. You know the kind of life you should be living—the kind of life you want to be living. But it seems out of reach. Beyond your grasp.

Take a moment right now to think of a character trait you would like to develop in your life. It may be courage, patience, or personal purity. Write it in the margin. Now, alongside that trait, write down the name of the person who, in your eyes, best exemplifies that particular strength. Why not stop right now, in the middle of reading this chapter, and pray about the trait and the name you have written down. Kneel before God's throne of grace and ask Him to grant you a double portion of that person's particular strength.

Do you need more patience? Who is the most patient, long-suffering person you know? Pray that with God's help you might become twice as patient as they are! Do you admire the wide-open spirit of hospitality in one of your friends? Ask the Lord for a double portion of that spirit! Make these requests an integral part of your prayer life. And if you'd like to encourage someone else, write a postcard to the person whose name came to mind. Tell him or her what you've prayed. That postcard may very well become one of their most treasured possessions.

Your Master, like Elisha's, has gone on into heaven. And while He is away, He has asked you to stand in His place, represent His name, and minister to His people. Like Elisha, you can't do that in your own strength . . . nor does God intend you to. He is the One "who is able to do immeasurably more than all we ask or imagine, according to his power that is at work within us" (Eph. 3:20). Power to live; power to serve. Power to be all that He wants you to be.

The Measure of Elisha's Ministry

(Read: Ephesians 4:1-16)

If you were Elisha, gifted with a double portion of Elijah's spirit and launched into your own career as a prophet, how would you begin to shape your ministry?

One of the first things you would probably do is pattern your life after that of your departed leader. Elisha now wore the mantle of Elijah. The "sons of the prophets" (2 Kings 2:15 NASB) paid him the homage they had previously reserved for Elijah alone. Elijah's work as a prophet had been dramatic and eminently successful. And now here you are with a double portion of that man's spirit! Why not try to become twice the Elijah that Elijah was? Sort of "out-Elijah" Elijah!

That's one course Elisha might have pursued. But he didn't.

Instead, the son of Shaphat developed his own unique style of ministry, geared to the times in which he lived and suited to his particular personality. Elisha never tried to imitate Elijah! It was not Elijah's mannerisms, style, or methods he had requested; it was Elijah's *strength and spirit*. Now, endowed with that strength, Elisha was free to utilize his own gifts—he was free to be himself.

Elijah was a prophet of fire and judgment; Elisha became a prophet of mercy and compassion.

Elijah was a man on the move; Elisha enjoyed the tranquility of home life.

Elijah's miracles were mainly destructive; Elisha's miracles were mainly constructive.

Elijah's ministry was one of stern warning; Elisha's ministry was one of tender teaching.

Elijah preferred solitude; Elisha preferred society.

What is the point of all these contrasts? Simply this: Elisha resisted what must have been a strong temptation to copy the style and methods of another man's ministry simply because it had worked for him. Instead, Elisha had the courage and creativity to be his own person, develop his own style, and search out that particular mode of ministering that was best suited to his own gifts, temperament, and personality.

How tempting it is to imitate others. You see someone with a creative idea that you admire, and you immediately try to become a clone of that individual. You work hard to adopt the methods, materials, and even the mannerisms of others simply because "it's working for them." And in the process you force yourself into a narrow, cliche-ridden box. Christ called you to Himself as a totally unique individual, with your own talents, outlook, and personality. Filled with His Spirit, you can be uniquely fruitful in your ministry for Him. What a boring world it would be if every fruit-bearing plant suddenly decided to produce apples simply because apples were popular.

Your infinitely creative God delights in diversity! That's why He created you exactly the way you are. He has gifted you with the ability to reflect the life of Jesus Christ in a way that no one else who ever walked the earth (or ever will) can hope to duplicate.

In a recent message to his congregation in Fullerton, California, Rev. Charles Swindoll revealed what he described as the turning point in his career. It came, he said, when he finally discovered that he was free to be himself. He didn't *have* to match someone else's style, duplicate someone else's results, or live up to someone else's expectations. Before God, he realized that he had the liberty to simply be Chuck Swindoll—a unique individual with a unique style all his own. When that truth finally dawned on him, it transformed his life—and his ministry. Across America, through his outreach from the pulpit, on radio and in literature, millions are grateful to the Lord for leading Pastor Swindoll to that discovery.

How about you? Have you found that freedom? Are you allowing Jesus Christ to exercise His love and grace in a creative way through your life and ministry? There are people whose lives Jesus Christ can touch uniquely through you that He simply could not reach through someone else.

Is God calling you to become an Elisha? Absolutely not. But He might be calling you to pray for a double portion of Elisha's spirit, and with it, the courage to be yourself.

Work It Through

1. Reread 1 Kings 19:19-21. Compare Elisha's request in verse 20 with the incident in Luke 9:57-62. Was Elisha faltering in the face of a prophetic call, or simply showing love and respect for his parents? What clue to this question do you pick up from the slaughtering of the oxen?

_____

_____

2. In what ways might Elisha have encouraged Elijah during his years of service to the prophet? Name three practical ways that you could be an encouragement to your minister, elder or a spiritual leader.

_____

_____

3. Some might argue that Elisha's request for a "double portion" of Elijah's spirit was selfish. Do you agree or disagree? Support your view.

_____

_____

4. In 1 Corinthians 11:1, Paul said, "Be imitators of me, just as I also am of Christ" (NASB). In what sense was the apostle asking the Corinthians to imitate him? How can you follow the example of a spiritual leader without compromising your own individual gifts, personality, and style of ministry?

_____

_____

5. Laboring for the Lord in obscurity, and ministering in the public eye both have their unique challenges. To which role have you been called? And how can you support and encourage those who labor in the opposite role?

_____

_____

NOTES

JONAH

Jonah may have never known what hit him. One minute he was sinking into a dark and angry sea and the next minute he was . . . well . . . somewhere else. *But where?* Had he already died? If so, where was he now? (It sure didn't feel like heaven.)

Swallowed alive! The thought of it is enough to bring chills to the spine. And yet, isn't that how it is with many of the circumstances of life. They come swooping out of nowhere and before you can run the other way or even register a complaint, you've been swallowed—consumed—engulfed!

And where is the Lord in all of this? Why does He allow the jaws of circumstances to clamp down on His children? Where is He when visibility suddenly drops to zero and the acid of anxiety begins to eat away at your sense of well-being? Jonah had to wrestle with that kind of slippery question. No doubt about it, he *had* disobeyed God. Was this, then, divine punishment? Was it a sign that God no longer cared what happened to His prophet?

Perhaps you have struggled with similar concerns in recent days. Your hardships may not match Jonah's encounter with "Jaws," but then sometimes a host of little problems—like a mob of hungry piranhas—can be equally distressing. Jonah learned a great deal about the grace and love of God during his incredible ordeal. As you read on . . . so can you.

The Rebellious Prophet (Jonah 1)

*V*ery little is known of Jonah's early life. Born into the household of Amittai, Jonah spends his early years in the Israelite town of Gath Hepher, north of what is today Nazareth in Galilee. (Note the error of the Lord's enemies in John 7:52!) Called of God to become a prophet, Jonah declared the Word of the Lord during the reign of Jeroboam II, the thirteenth king of Israel.

At the beginning of the book that bears his name, Jonah is commissioned by God to deliver an ultimatum to Nineveh, the violent capitol of Israel's archenemy, Assyria. Unwilling to obey this summons, the prophet flees in a ship sailing in the opposite direction. A violent storm at sea reveals Jonah's rebellion to the ship's terrified crew. Hurled overboard into the raging sea, Jonah's career as a prophet appears to be short-lived. But God prepares a unique "rescue vessel" to swallow up the unwilling prophet and take him on a three-day voyage . . . back into the will of God.

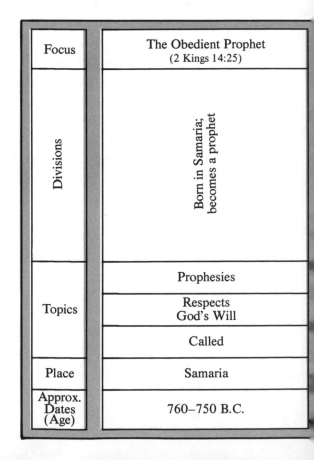

Focus	The Obedient Prophet (2 Kings 14:25)
Divisions	Born in Samaria; becomes a prophet
Topics	Prophesies
	Respects God's Will
	Called
Place	Samaria
Approx. Dates (Age)	760–750 B.C.

The Repentant and Effective Prophet (Jonah 2,3)

*I*nside the great fish, Jonah's prayer life is renewed. He prays, quotes from the Psalms, cries to God for mercy and finally agrees to obey the Lord's command. Once again the Lord speaks to the fish, which promptly deposits the repentant prophet onto dry land. Once again the word of the Lord comes to Jonah with the command: "Go to Nineveh!" This time the prophet loses no time in obeying, and promptly begins the 500-mile trek to the great city on the banks of the Tigris. Once inside, Jonah delivers his one-sentence sermon and witnesses one of the greatest revivals of all time. The entire city, from the peasant on the street to the king on the throne, turns from its wicked ways and pleads with God for mercy. God hears from heaven, cancels His sentence of doom, and proves Himself to be the God of the Gentiles as well as the Jews.

The Instructed Prophet (Jonah 4)

*D*ramatic as the results of Jonah's preaching may be, they are not sufficient to warm the prophet's heart toward the perennial enemies of his people. Instead of rejoicing, Jonah becomes angry at the Lord for His mercy toward the Assyrians. Jonah is so bitter that he begs God to take away his life. He cannot bear the thought of living in a world with forgiven Assyrians.

Sitting to the east of the city in a homemade shelter, Jonah waits to see if perhaps God will change His mind and destroy the Ninevites after all. As he swelters in the Mid-East sun, God causes a vine to grow up over his head to shade him. But Jonah's great pleasure is short-lived. The next morning a divinely-sent worm destroys the vine, leaving Jonah overwhelmed with anger and self-pity. God uses the incident as a graphic object lesson to His servant. Jonah pities a mere vine; God feels pity for tens of thousands of Ninevites who have not yet had the opportunity to respond to His love.

The Rebellious Prophet (Jonah 1:1–17)	The Repentant Prophet (Jonah 2:1–10)	The Effective Prophet (Jonah 3:1–10)	The Instructed Prophet (Jonah 4:1–11)
Disobeys God; flees in a ship	Swallowed by a fish; repents and worships	Preaches in Nineveh; witnesses revival	Questions God's grace and mercy
Protests	Prays	Preaches	Pouts
Rejects God's Plan	Receives God's Discipline	Reveals God's Message	Resents God's Grace
Disciplined	Delivered	Repentant	Reproved
Sea	Sea Monster	City of Nineveh	Suburb of Nineveh
760—750 B.C.		760—750 B.C.	

The God Who Won't Let Go

(Read Jonah 1-2)

The command came with ringing clarity: "Go to the great city of Nineveh and preach against it, because its wickedness has come up before me" (Jonah 1:2).

There it was. No room for loopholes, speculations, or alternate interpretations. You couldn't spiritualize a command like that.

To turn from this command would be nothing less than direct disobedience and raw rebellion. Jonah knew that. And yet he turned anyway. The Lord's assignment for the prophet was to have taken him due *east*. Jonah packed his flight bag and headed due *west*. First to Joppa and then on toward Tarshish—at the very edge of the known world. It was as cold and deliberate an action as a man could take. Verse three says that "Jonah ran away from the Lord" and "sailed for Tarshish to flee from the Lord."

It didn't really matter where the ship was headed. Jonah merely wanted to put some distance between himself and the Lord.

What must the prophet have been thinking? Did he really believe he could climb aboard a ship and sail away from God's presence? Wasn't he familiar with the words of King David?

> Where can I go from your Spirit?
> Where can I flee from your presence?
> If I rise on the wings of the dawn,
> if I settle on the far side of the sea,
> even there your hand will guide me,
> your right hand will hold me fast.
> Ps. 139:7,9,10.

Surely a prophet of the Lord would have known these things. Perhaps Jonah subscribed to the popular notion that the spirit of prophecy lived in Israel alone. If only he could break away from Israelite soil he could escape "the word of the Lord" (Jonah 1:2) that had given him such a repugnant mission. Nineveh, after all, was the capital of Israel's archenemy Assyria. Jonah needed no reminder that the Assyrians were among the most cruel and violent of peoples ever to inhabit the earth.

"There are other prophets," Jonah may have reasoned, "other men who can speak as clearly as I. Let God send one of them if

He's so concerned about warning the Assyrians. If I deliberately disobey Him and oppose His will, it will surely disqualify me for the job. God will *have* to find a more reliable spokesman. Then He'll probably forget all about me and let me go my way."

How little Jonah knew of God's love. What the prophet failed to realize was this: the minister is as important to God as the ministry. God is not only concerned with His work, He is concerned for His workers. Of course God's heart grieved over the wicked Ninevites. Of course He was concerned for the 120,000 Ninevite children who did not know of His love (Jonah 4:11). But God was also concerned about something else. One of His servants had gone A.W.O.L. from the pathway of obedience and blessing, and was blundering into paths of bitterness and rebellion. Jonah's life was headed for disaster, and God loved him too much not to intervene. Jonah never reckoned with the tenacity of God's love. The Lord would simply not let him go.

Notice how God takes the initiative throughout the first chapter. Verse four says that *"the Lord sent a great wind on the sea...."* And in verse 17, *"the Lord provided a great fish to swallow Jonah."*

The storm was God's doing. The sailor's lot fell on Jonah because God *caused* it to fall on Jonah. The lord *sent* the great fish that swallowed the prophet. It was no fluke, no coincidence— God did it to Jonah.

But why? To punish him for his impudence? To show him once and for all who's the boss? Was the storm simply God's knee-jerk reflex of frustration and anger because the prophet refused to listen?

The context says otherwise. God loved this headstrong servant of His. As a matter of fact, Jonah was the only prophet in the Bible to whom Jesus directly compared Himself (Matt. 12:40). When God sent distress and hardship into Jonah's life it was not to *punish* him as an offender, but to *discipline* him as a well-loved child. Certainly God could have sent someone else to Nineveh. But then Jonah would have missed out on a priceless learning experience that God had planned for his life. God wanted Jonah to grow out of his prejudiced and narrow view of God's grace. He wanted to share with His servant something of God's heartbeat for *all men*—regardless of race, color or nationality.

The second chapter of Jonah reveals that God's discipline had its desired effect. The prophet did not curse God or lapse into despair within the great fish. Not at all. Jonah *prayed*. He quoted from the Psalms, he cried to God for mercy, he repented of his rebellious heart, he remembered his calling as a prophet, he renewed his vow to become God's spokesman (Jonah 2:9). Only hours before he had tried to flee from God's presence. Now he longed for it desperately.

Because of God's discipline in his life, Jonah came back. He was restored. God gave him a new commission. Instead of moldering for the rest of his years on the piers of Tarshish, aimlessly scanning the horizon, Jonah became the key human figure in perhaps history's greatest revival. He was back on the cutting edge of God's program for the world.

That's the intent of God's discipline. Not to damage, but to heal. Not to badger or bully, but to restore and renew.

The writer of Hebrews sought to impress this truth on his readers who were staggering under some particularly heavy discipline in their lives. As a result of their circumstances, they were beginning to waver in their commitment to Christ, and were losing heart. "You have forgotten that word of encouragement that addresses you as sons," he wrote. " 'My son, do not make light of the Lord's discipline, and do not lose heart when he rebukes you, because the Lord disciplines those whom he loves and he punishes everyone he accepts as a son.' *Endure hardship as discipline; God is treating you as sons.* For what son is not disciplined by his father?" (Heb. 12:5-7, italics added.)

Every true believer faces discipline. Far from it being a sign of God's anger or rejection, His discipline is the hallmark of His tender love. Though He may allow a broad range of hardships to enter the life of a believer, His objective is always the same: "God disciplines us for our good, that we may share in his holiness. . . . It produces a harvest of righteousness and peace for those who have been trained by it" (Heb. 12:10,11).

Sometimes discipline is hard to view that way. In the midst of struggle, perplexity, or pain, it is often difficult to grasp the fact that God is demonstrating His love—that He is drawing you to Himself.

Perhaps you are at a point in your life where the words of Jonah in chapter two express the feelings of your heart:

> The engulfing waters threatened me,
>   the deep surrounded me . . .
> To the roots of the mountains I sank down.
>
> Jonah 2:5,6

Jonah was on his way down, down, down. Into hopeless, helpless darkness. But then—at the blackest moment of the prophet's life—something clicked in his spirit. With suffocating seaweed wrapped around his head, and a prayer of confession on his lips, Jonah moved from willful pride to open surrender.

> When my life was ebbing away,
>   I remembered you, Lord,
> and my prayer rose to you,
>   to your holy temple
>
> Jonah 2:7

In a matter of hours Jonah had been delivered from his pit of despair and was on his way to new exploits for the Lord.

So often God is forced to use discipline in our lives—not because He wants to, but because He knows it is the only way we will ever hear and respond. C.S. Lewis once called pain "God's megaphone." We run so fast and hard and long that we seldom give God time to speak to us in that "still, small voice" He loves to use with His children. If only we would slow down and spend time alone with Him and His Word, He could speak to us gently about those needy areas of our lives. But sometimes He never gets the chance! And so, rather than let us run headlong into disaster (He loves us too much for that), He sends the dark clouds, He sends the storm, and if he must . . . He sends the "whale."

Are you facing an area of struggle or heartache in your life today? Could it be that God wants to use that very circumstance as a "megaphone" to get your attention? When was the last time you

The Great (Re) Commission
(Read: Jonah 3-4)

gave God the opportunity to speak to you? Why not slow down for awhile today . . . or this evening . . . and speak to your heavenly Father about potential "Ninevehs" in your life. And take time to praise Him—for a love that refuses to let you go.

The great fish is a scene-stealer in the book of Jonah. The mere mention of the prophet's name conjures up vivid imagery of storm-tossed seas and great open-jawed "whales."

A closer look, however, reveals that the famous fish is really a rather minor character in the whole drama. Obviously, God could have used any number of means to transport the prophet from the Tarshish-bound freighter to the land of Israel.

Some have gone so far as to say that the most remarkable line in the whole book has nothing whatever to do with the fish. Consider the first two verses of chapter three:

"Then the word of the Lord came to Jonah a *second* time: 'Go to the great city of Nineveh and proclaim to it the message I give you' " (Jonah 3:1).

The word of the Lord came a second time! God gave Jonah another opportunity to serve Him. In fact, He repeated exactly the same commission He had given to Jonah in the first place. It was as if the whole incident of rebellion and repentance had never occurred. The need in Nineveh was as great as ever. God still had a message for the Ninevites. And in spite of everything that had taken place, Jonah, the son of Amittai, was still God's chosen instrument to deliver that crucial message.

It was like an echo in time. God once again held out an astounding opportunity to His servant, but this time, the results were vastly different. Jonah—a recent graduate of "Whale University"— "obeyed the word of the Lord and went to Nineveh" (Jonah 3:3).

Jonah is not the only Bible character who looked like a poor investment risk for God's time and resources. The apostle Paul was ready to remove John Mark's name from the missionary roster simply because the young man wavered in his commitment and returned home mid-voyage (Acts 15:36-40). But at least Mark had given it a try! How much less desirable is a missionary that openly rebels and does the opposite of what God tells him to do. If you were in a place of responsibility on a mission board, would you have voted to recommission Jonah after his "fish fiasco"?

And yet . . . "the word of the Lord came to Jonah a second time."

Perhaps Jonah exhibited such a dramatic change of attitude that God felt compelled to give the prophet another chance. Perhaps Jonah was now so deeply in love with his task and felt such soul-stirring compassion for the Ninevites that the councils of heaven decreed that he should go.

What does chapter 4 say about Jonah's response to the electrifying revival that swept the streets of Nineveh like a summer storm? Did Jonah rejoice over those incredible results?

Not exactly. Scripture says that Jonah "was greatly displeased and became angry" (Jonah 4:1). Paraphrasing verses two and three, Jonah exploded at the Lord and said, "I knew this would happen! Lord, why do you think I rebelled in the first place? I *knew* what kind of God you are—loving and merciful—and if these vile Assyrians repented, I feared that You would forgive them all. And now You have! Why don't You just kill me and end this miserable life of mine? I'm more good to You dead than alive."

Jonah obeyed the Lord this second time, but his attitude was as bitter and resentful as ever. Even after God had used him in such a mighty way, Jonah sulked and pouted and complained. If God did not give up on Jonah after his initial rebellion, then surely He could be expected to wash His hands of this stubborn man now! Talk about a rude, ungrateful individual. And yet, read through the rest of the chapter and see how God handles this situation. See how gently He reasons with His servant; see how He appeals to the prophet's heart.

What a loving, patient God! A God who refused to give up on Jonah after the prophet disobeyed. A God who looked for and found the most effective form of discipline for Jonah's life, and used it to show Jonah the folly of his ways and his need for repentance. Though the prophet's heart was far from perfect, God used Jonah's witness to move the very heart of a nation.

Jonah is the book for people who feel they have failed too often for God to use them. Jonah's presence in the Bible is a startling affirmation of the grace and patience that God extends toward His weak, failing children.

Jonah obeyed and trusted God even though his heart was not right toward Him. *And God accepted that service.* It was as though the Lord was saying, "Listen Jonah, *you* obey My word and let Me work on those bad attitudes. Let *Me* work on those weak areas of your heart. With My help,Jonah, you can grow— and as you're growing I'll use you to accomplish great things for Me."

You will often be tempted to say to the Lord, "Yes, Lord, I *will* serve You. But I've failed You so miserably in the past that I have to work on a few things first. Let me get my life straightened out a little and then I'll put myself in Your hands." *It will never work!* You cannot change your own attitudes. You can't strengthen your own weaknesses. You can't force your own emotions into a "spiritual" mold. Only the Spirit of God can do that! Only He can transform lives. And He will, if you will humbly place your life under His complete control. If you will only say, "Lord, You know I'm not what I could be—I'm definitely not what I should be. But thank You that I'm also not what I used to be. And with Your help and strength, I will live for You *today.*"

That's what the apostle Paul said to the believers in Philippi: "Not that I have already obtained all this, or have already been made perfect, but I press on to take hold of that for which Christ Jesus took hold of me. Brothers, I do not consider myself yet to have taken hold of it. But one thing I do: Forgetting what is behind and straining toward what is ahead, I press on toward the goal to win the prize for which God has called me heavenward in Christ Jesus" (Phil. 3:12-14).

God can use you. Just as you are. In spite of your failures. In spite of your emotional struggles. In spite of your "poor track record." He knows your frame; he remembers that you are made of dust (Ps. 103:14). And even now He can work through your life to encourage other believers and to bring others who do not know Him into the family of God.

But you have to give Him the chance. You have to stop running and start listening for His loving and patient voice.

Three hundred years ago, the hymn writer Joachim Neander penned these promising words:

JONAH

*Praise to the Lord, who doth prosper thy work
and defend thee;
Surely His goodness and mercy here daily
attend thee.
Ponder anew what the Almighty can do,
If with His love He befriend thee!*

Praise be to His name . . . He *has* befriended you!

Work It Through

1. When Jonah objected so strongly to going to Nineveh, why didn't God simply allow the prophet to run away, and then select someone else?

_____

_____

2. Why did Jonah seek to "flee from the Lord"? Do you think he actually supposed he could run away from the presence of the Lord?

_____

_____

3. In his prayer from within the fish's stomach, Jonah recited his experiences and emotions to the Lord. How does telling the Lord exactly what you are feeling help you in your prayer life?

_____

_____

4. Does the repetition of God's commission to Jonah in 3:1,2 offer any encouragement for your life? Explain how and why.

_____

_____

5. In chapter 4 Jonah demonstrates an unloving attitude toward the Ninevites. What is your chief responsibility when God urges you to speak to a particular person about faith in Christ?

_____

_____

6. How does God's use of discipline in chapter 4 differ from the discipline He employs in chapter 1? Can you see any parallels between the way God deals with Jonah in chapter 4 and the way He has been dealing with you in recent days?

_____

_____

NOTES

Daniel

"I have this strange feeling that something is going to happen . . ."

Did you ever hear anyone say that? Have you said it yourself? And did that "something" ever really come about . . . or did you forget about it in ten minutes?

Talk about a "sense of impending disaster" is usually just that . . . talk. Crisis gives notoriously little warning before it bursts into your life. It doesn't call ten minutes before it arrives. It refuses to knock politely and wait for an invitation. More likely, it simply rams the door off its hinges and there it is. Unannounced, unexpected, unwelcome, and unwilling to go away. Now . . . what do you do with it? Does it stagger you . . . or strengthen you? Does it ruin you . . . or refine you? Does it plunge you into despair . . . or draw you closer to your Lord?

Important questions. Important not just for you, but for others as well. The way you handle sudden crises has a lot to say about the reality of your faith in Jesus Christ. You may talk a good faith, but the way you move through stressful situations in your life reveals to every watching eye the actual fibre of your faith. Is it just window dressing, or is it an inner power that gives you peace and perspective in the midst of pain? That's the kind of faith that compels people to sit up and take notice. Although Daniel's faith was severely tested all through his life, it stood strong and eventually compelled all of Babylon to seek the Source of his strength.

Daniel's LIFE IN SUMMARY

Daniel, Exile to Babylon

Born into a family of nobility during the reign of good King Josiah, Daniel evidently enjoyed the warmth and security of a godly home. His parents may have been among those touched by Josiah's great national revival. The Book of the Law had been discovered by the young king and the power of its renewed impact was being felt across Judah.

In his early teenage years, however, Daniel witnesses his nation's shocking retreat from the righteous reforms of Josiah. The little hope aroused in godly hearts by Judah's brief repentance is quickly snuffed out as first Jehoahaz and then Jehoiakim steer the nation toward inevitable judgment and destruction.

Nebuchadnezzar's conquering army loots the temple of Solomon and carries away a number of choice young Hebrew men to serve in the Babylonian court. Daniel, torn from home, family, and everything familiar, finds himself numbered among those captives.

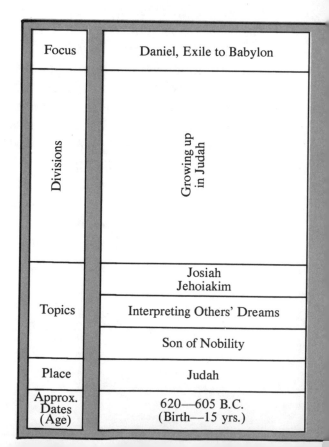

Focus	Daniel, Exile to Babylon
Divisions	Growing up in Judah
Topics	Josiah Jehoiakim
	Interpreting Others' Dreams
	Son of Nobility
Place	Judah
Approx. Dates (Age)	620—605 B.C. (Birth—15 yrs.)

Daniel, Counselor to Kings

Immediately upon entering Babylon, young Daniel's convictions are put to the test. Refusing to violate Jewish dietary laws, Daniel and his three friends rely on God to help them thrive on a vegetarian diet. Three years after his arrival, the young Hebrew faces yet another crisis when all the wise men of Babylon—himself included—are threatened with death for their inability to describe and interpret Nebuchadnezzar's dream. Once again relying on the Lord, Daniel accomplishes this task and is promoted to a high position within the kingdom.

While Daniel pursues his administrative career in the Babylonian government during the reigns of Nebuchadnezzar and Belshazzar, he is given at least two more opportunities to interpret divine messages. For Nebuchadnezzar, it is a dream of future world powers. For the king's son, Belshazzar, the prophet literally sees the handwriting on the wall: Babylon and its reckless king are doomed.

Daniel's civil service career continues to flourish under the new world power—Medo-Persia. King Darius finds Daniel so highly qualified and of such an "excellent spirit" that he promotes the elderly Jew to one of the three top posts in the empire. Jealous over the honor and favor accorded to this Hebrew, a number of Daniel's fellow administrators plot to overthrow him. Their plans appear to succeed in spite of the king's best efforts to save his trustworthy minister. Daniel is sentenced to certain death in a den of ravenous lions. What a shock for Darius (and Daniel's enemies) when Daniel is discovered alive and unscathed after a night among the beasts.

Daniel's unshakable faithfulness, even in the face of death, results in great honor for the name of his God. The prophet continues to prosper through the reigns of both Darius the Mede and Cyrus the Persian. As he nears death, Daniel experiences additional apocalyptic visions.

Daniel, Counselor to Kings				Daniel, Counselor to Kings	
Training in the Babylonian Court	Interprets Nebuchadnezzar's image dream	Promotion to high office	Interprets Nebuchadnezzar's tree dream	Predicts Babylon's doom	Stays loyal to God urder Persian rule
Nebuchadnezzar				Belshazzar	Darius, Cyrus
Interpreting Others' Dreams				Interpreting Daniel's Dreams (chs. 7—12)	
Prophet and Statesman				Prophet and Statesman	
Babylonia				Babylonia	
605–539 B.C. (15–82 yrs.)				539—530 B.C. (82 yrs.–Death)	

Courage and Conviction

(Read: Daniel 1)

There was probably very little time to say good-bye.

As the intended captives were torn from their families to begin the long march, two visual images must have burned in their hearts: the anguish-filled faces of their loved ones, and that last glimpse of the city God had abandoned to its fate—beloved Jerusalem. A fleeting glance . . . and it was all behind them. They were on their way to a future filled with dark mysteries. Destination: Babylon.

Nebuchadnezzar might have called the operation "skimming the cream." But for the nation of Judah, the arrival of the Crown Prince of Babylon at the gates of Jerusalem was an omen of her final hour. The beginning of the end.

Nebuchadnezzar had no intention of destroying Judah's capital. Not yet, anyway. He simply wanted to make a point. In case the Jews had other ideas, he wanted to remind them that Babylon ruled the world. Judah was simply a vassal state. To reinforce his point, the warrior/prince helped himself to some of the gold reserves in Solomon's temple. But that wasn't all. When Nebuchadnezzar "skimmed Judah's cream," he also skimmed the cream of Judah's youth. The order went out to the chief of his court officials to "bring in some of the Israelites from the royal family and the nobility . . . qualified to serve in the king's palace" (Dan. 1 3,4).

Try to identify with the emotional upheaval—the wrenching inner pain—of these teen-agers as they were swept along the ancient trade route with the conquering Babylonians. Feel the sorrow and remorse . . . the anger and fear that must have brought tears to their eyes and knots to their stomachs. Their homes, their families, their proud temple all behind them—perhaps forever. Familiar streets, familiar faces, best friends and sweethearts—gone! How powerless they must have felt. Judah's weak, shattered army could not help them. And ahead? A strange, alien city in a land so far away it might as well be the moon. Would God actually allow them to live out their lives in that forbidden and foreboding city, rumored to be filled with bizarre temples and teeming idolatry? Unthinkable!

Nevertheless, these were intelligent young men that Nebuchadnezzar had garnered from Judah. The *summa cum laude* of the nation's youth. And given time, when necessity demands, even the unthinkable becomes thinkable. There had to be a facing of reality. As they sat around the soldiers' campfires night after night, listening to the wild confusion of a thousand foreign conversations, these elite youngsters must have soberly considered their futures. How would they face life in this new world capital? How would they make the best of a seemingly disastrous situation?

Undoubtedly, a number of the young men considered *compromise*. There were worse things in life than living in the very center of world commerce, culture and power. After all, they had been handpicked by the king's chief court officials for a lifetime of royal service. So how could a young Hebrew get ahead in such a world? How could he blend in with the foreign lifestyle, make the right contacts, and start rising toward the top?

Daniel, one of the captives, was also doing some heavy thinking. But Daniel's thoughts were taking him in a different direction. Daniel loved the Lord, and at the very core of his being he was forming a resolve that would mark him for a lifetime. A resolve that would shape his destiny.

Verse eight of chapter one says that Daniel "made up his mind" (NASB), or "purposed in his heart" (KJV) that he would not "defile himself with the royal food and wine." No matter what happened, he would not compromise his commitment to God and to the Law of his God. The matter of food and drink was only a part of a much greater commitment. Daniel was going to live a life of complete loyalty to Jehovah—no matter where he lived, no matter who objected. Making such a decision might bring deep humiliation. Daniel was prepared for that. It might mean a life locked away in the black depths of an unspeakable dungeon. Then again, his "hosts" might save trouble by simply running him through with a sword.

But Daniel had a resolve. An unshakable purpose. Literally, he "set upon his heart" not to defile himself. It was like a firebrand on his soul. Come what may, God would remain first. Pleasing Him would be more important than pleasing men. Period. As Daniel walked through the massive gates of Babylon, he could do so with a measure of peace. The peace of a man whose lines are drawn, whose course is set. The peace of a man who has surrendered his fate into the hands of God.

Consider for a moment what might have happened if the Hebrew teen-ager had merely drifted into Babylon with a vague set of principles. What if he had waited awhile to form his convictions and establish the purpose of his heart? Would there have been a book of Daniel? Would his loosely held beliefs have survived the acid test that was Babylon? Would lukewarm convictions have enabled Daniel to resist the heady allurements and enticements which Babylon presented? Would a half-hearted love for the God of Israel have motivated Daniel to face the furnace of fire . . . or the den of lions?

There is a vast difference between holding a belief and entering into a conviction. One is a matter of the intellect, the other a matter of the will. One says, "I am convinced." The other says, "I am committed." A man may argue for his beliefs, but he will *die* for his convictions. A belief is something held in the hand. If the pressure is great enough, if the storm is fierce enough, a belief may become dislodged from the grip and slip away in the current. A conviction, however, is held in the *heart*. It is stitched into the fabric of one's very being. No pressure, no storm— no matter how violent— can destroy a conviction without destroying something of the one who holds it. A conviction is nothing more than a belief with its boots on . . . ready to march, ready to fight, ready to die.

Jesus Christ calls for convictions among His believing people. A driving, inner purpose of life that can stand strong in the withering blast of trial, that can say "No!" to the sensual enticements of a Babylon, that can stay on course in the face of indifference, sarcasm, or open hostility. No mere intellectual belief can stand up to the acid test of discipleship. No lukewarm love will go to the lions' den rather than betray its Loved One. Only a well-defined, strongly fixed commitment can face that kind of resistance and come out a winner.

Paul expressed that sort of conviction many times during his long, turbulent ministry. *"I know* whom I have believed," he wrote to his young friend Timothy (2 Tim. 1:12). *"One thing I do,"* he penned to the Philippians, "Forgetting what is behind and straining toward what is ahead, I press on toward the goal to win the prize for which God has called me heavenward in Christ Jesus" (Phil. 3:13,14). In the same letter, he described how he endured tremendous loss, from a human perspective, in the process of reaching toward that burning, all-consuming goal of his life: "I want to know Christ and the power of his resurrection" (Phil. 3:7–10).

Like Daniel, Paul faced humiliation, danger, and incredible persecution. And like Daniel, he was able to move ahead through life with a calm assurance that defied logic. There was a steady, unmistakable "blip" on Paul's inner radar screen that enabled him to fly on course through storm after storm even when he couldn't see what lay before him. Paul didn't merely "hold beliefs"—he was "consumed by convictions." He knew what he wanted in life. His eyes of faith were locked on a goal.

On the first day of a very large journalism class I was attending, the professor began by saying, "I want to go around the room this morning and have each of you give your name and something that is *different* about you. We'll begin with this young man sitting in the front row."

He was pointing at *me!* I was aghast. In that split second I recognized a priceless opportunity to share a simple word about my faith in the Lord Jesus, and the difference He had made in my life. It was a tailor-made platform for witnessing. But the words wouldn't come. All I could do was stammer out my name.

"Come now," said the professor, "surely there is *something* different about you that you could share with us." I could feel the heat radiating from my face, but I could say nothing. The thought of speaking out in front of a potentially hostile audience left me petrified. In a matter of seconds, the opportunity passed.

For the rest of the class hour, I was sick with humiliation and regret. It seemed like I could hear a cock crowing three times in the distance. After the class was over, I approached the professor.

"Uh . . . I thought of something about myself, sir. If you could give me another chance . . . " He seemed noncommittal. At our

DANIEL

next class meeting he started right into his lecture and I almost breathed a sigh of relief. But then he stopped.

"Before we begin today, one of your classmates has something he would like to say to you. *Come on up front, young man.*"

Looking back now, I can't even remember what I said. But before I sat down, the professor said, "I want to see you in my office after class." Oh boy. Now I had done it. Proselyting in a university classroom. At least the Lord had given me another opportunity to identify with Him. When I stepped into the professor's office later that day, he surprised me with a smile. It seems his grandfather had given him a Christian book . . . had I read it? And this thing about becoming a Christian . . . well, his wife and daughter had just become Christians. He was puzzled. What was it all about?

In this age of crumbling foundations and shifting values, millions long for some kind of deep, unifying truth that will give meaning to their lives. For this reason, countless thousands are plunging into the chaos of cultism—desperately looking for *something* to grasp, something to give their lives hope, security, purpose.

When a man or woman takes a strong stand for his faith in Jesus Christ, people will sit up and take notice. Many may ridicule this "narrow-mindedness," others will try to find fault. But all the same, they will be watching . . . wondering. *"This person seems so serene, so secure, so stable. He really trusts in the Bible . . . she really believes that Jesus is alive. My life seems so directionless, so empty . . . could there really be something to this kind of Christianity . . . ?"*

Is your Christian life marked by beliefs . . . or convictions? Is there a need this week to get alone with your Lord and talk about the purpose for which He has left you on earth?

Perhaps the old hymn writer said it best:

"Dare to be a Daniel, dare to stand alone
Dare to have a purpose firm, dare to make it known."

Courage and Consistency

(Read: Daniel 2, 6)

Daniel was a man of *purpose*. But perhaps He is best remembered as a man of *prayer*.

Vital as it is to have a strong, inner purpose and direction for your life, it is all useless and empty unless that purpose is powered by prayer. Having a purpose without an active dependence on God is like climbing into a car and sliding the gearshift lever into "drive." Your purpose is set; your goal is fixed; you are fully committed to move forward. Your face is a picture of strong will and determination as you gaze through your windshield at distant horizons. The only trouble is, you aren't going anywhere. Not until you start the engine and push down the gas pedal. Prayer is like the ignition and power that give purpose its dynamic and forward thrust.

Prayer was an inseparable part of Daniel's life—his natural recourse in time of stress as well as his daily habit of life.

When Daniel was an old, gray-headed man, he was hauled before the Persian authorities and sentenced to die. This was not the first time the faithful exile had faced the death penalty, but as he was being marched away to a den of hungry lions, the old prophet must have wondered if it would be his last.

No doubt about it; Daniel had deliberately broken the law of the land. In spite of his impressive credentials as a Persian public servant, Daniel had refused to bow to his government's latest edict. He would not pray to King Darius; he would pray to his Lord God, just as he had done every day since he was a child.

Three times every day, as was his habit, Daniel would retire to an upper room, open the window that faced toward Jerusalem, and pray to the Lord he loved. He had done it for years—decades. He was so consistent in his prayer life that his enemies could trap him in the act with the greatest of ease. They knew where Daniel would be and what he would be doing at three specific times each and every day. Folks around Daniel's house knew they could set their watches by the sight of that old man kneeling in front of his window.

Three times daily, Daniel renewed his commitment to God. Three times daily, he sought confirmation from his Shepherd that he was on the right path.

Daniel was a man of purpose. But Daniel did not seek to power his life with that purpose. Instead, he sought to power his purpose through prayer.

Many believers look back on a time when they took a definite stand for Jesus Christ. Perhaps it was at a church meeting, in a neighbor's house, at their bedside as a little child, or in a noisy student union on campus. Those are wonderful moments of spiritual perspective. No one can ever take away the joyful memories of a commitment to Jesus Christ. Nevertheless, *the Christian life was never meant to go forward solely on the strength of a one-time commitment;* strength flows from a living relationship with the Son of God.

Imagine you could go back in time and visit with Daniel on a bustling street in downtown Babylon. Get alone with him for a few minutes; ask him about his relationship with God; probe the spiritual realities in his life. What would his response likely be? Would he ramble and reminisce, taking you back to that night when, as a teen-ager, he sat in front of a Babylonian army campfire? Would he look back on that night when he prayed with his friends for the interpretation of the king's dream? Would he have to blow the dust off decade-old memories in order to recall a time when God was at work in his life? Or would Daniel be able to relate freshly answered prayers . . . new insights from God's Word . . . recent miracles in his daily walk with God?

And what if Daniel turned the tables and asked the same question of you? Could you respond, "Let me tell you about the insight the Lord gave me from the Psalms this morning . . . You know, I had the most encouraging conversation with God this afternoon . . . Yesterday God answered my prayers in a most remarkable and unexpected way . . . ."

People often speak of Daniel's great courage. As if he had to reach way down within himself and pull from the bottom of the well some latent, superhuman quality. I don't think that's a very accurate picture. Daniel was no different from the rest of us. He wasn't bionic. He didn't wear the uniform of a Supersaint underneath his robes. Daniel was simply a man who experienced a loving, consistent walk with God. Day after day. Year in, year out. In his teens. In his 20's and 30's and 40's. All the way into his 90's.

When a crisis came, he was ready. He had God's perspective. He was refreshed by God's presence. The communication lines between Daniel's house and heaven were wide open. It wasn't that Daniel was a man of great *courage*. It was rather that he was a man of great *consistency*. He was a man who leaned hard on God.

What if the word went out in your neighborhood to round up those suspected of worshiping the Lord God? Would the authorities be able to find enough evidence to convict you? Would they be able to trap you like they trapped Daniel, simply because your life was so consistent? Or would they go right by your door?

You may never have to face a blazing furnace or a den of lions because of the consistency of your prayer life. Your faithfulness may never make the headlines. Nevertheless, as you rub shoulders with friends, family and associates on a day-to-day basis, they'll know if you've consistently sought God's strength or if you have been trying to live on the strength of yesterday's commitment. You won't have to say a word. It will be written all over your life.

Work It Through

1. What were two ways in which Daniel demonstrated his loyalty to the Lord even in the middle of a pagan culture like Babylon? How can you follow his model as you face the pressures and temptations in your daily life?

_____

_____

2. What is the difference between a *belief* and a *conviction*? How can a person transform his beliefs into convictions?

_____

_____

3. According to 1 Peter 3:15,16, what are two possible results you should expect if you hold firm convictions in your heart?

_____

_____

4. What are the possible benefits of setting a specific time each day for prayer? What are the potential pitfalls?

_____

_____

5. If you are a timid person by nature, how can the quality of courage grow out of a *consistent* walk with the Lord?

_____

_____

6. In chapter 6, Daniel deliberately disobeyed his government's edict and was promptly arrested. Would it have been wiser for Daniel to "moderate" his prayer habits—praying silently, praying in the closet—instead of openly defying Persia's ban on prayer? Why or why not? At what point should a Christian ever consider breaking one of the laws of his government?

_____

_____

NOTES

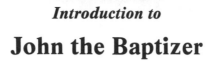

John the Baptizer

WANTED: Young man to serve in position as king's herald. No pay. No housing. Locusts and wild honey available for food, but not provided. Applicant must be willing to work long hours, face fierce opposition and grave dangers. If successful in meeting stringent qualifications of position, applicant's services will soon no longer be required.

If God had put an ad like that in the Sunday paper, how many responses do you suppose He would have received?

Obviously, God didn't *have* to buy space in the classifieds to find a forerunner for Jesus Christ. It wasn't necessary for Him to phone a dozen employment agencies or conduct interviews on college campuses. God had His man all picked out . . . before man ever walked on earth . . . before a single star shone in the blackness of space. John didn't enlist; he was *drafted*. And he loved it. Before it was all over, the King's herald would say, "[My] joy is complete" (John 3:29). Even though fulfilling his mission meant working himself out of a job, John the Baptist was supremely happy.

But wait! Does the story end there? Is the position of King's herald still open today? Are *you* a potential candidate for the job? The answer may surprise you.

John's Preparation
(Luke 1:5-80)

*W*hile Zacharias performs his priestly duties in the temple of the Lord, he is startled by the sudden appearance of the angel Gabriel. The heavenly messenger announces that Zacharias and his barren wife Elizabeth will soon become the parents of a son! The boy, to be named John, will be great in the eyes of the Lord and will serve as the forerunner of Israel's long-awaited Messiah.

True to Gabriel's words, John is born to the elderly couple and filled with the Holy Spirit from the day of his birth. Brought up under the strict vows of a Nazarite, John leaves home in his early adulthood to live in the lonely deserts of Judea. He clothes himself with a garment of camel's hair and a leather belt—the same kind of clothing worn by the Old Testament prophet Elijah—and subsists on a diet of locusts and wild honey as he awaits the day of his public appearance to Israel.

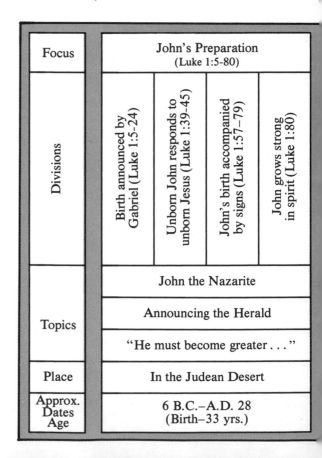

Focus	John's Preparation (Luke 1:5-80)			
Divisions	Birth announced by Gabriel (Luke 1:5-24)	Unborn John responds to unborn Jesus (Luke 1:39-45)	John's birth accompanied by signs (Luke 1:57-79)	John grows strong in spirit (Luke 1:80)
Topics	John the Nazarite			
	Announcing the Herald			
	"He must become greater . . ."			
Place	In the Judean Desert			
Approx. Dates Age	6 B.C.–A.D. 28 (Birth–33 yrs.)			

John's Presentation
(Luke 3:1-22)

*W*hen the time for John's appearance arrives, he bursts onto the scene with dramatic force and boundless energy. Because of his wild appearance and unusual message, crowds flock to see and hear John at the Jordan River. Many respond to his call for repentance and express their change of heart by being baptized.

Like the prophets of old, John sternly warns Israel's religious and political leaders: Messiah is coming to judge and to rule! One day as he is baptizing, John meets the Messiah face to face, and at Jesus' request, baptizes Him as well.

As the ministry of Jesus widens, the ministry of the Baptizer wanes. Several of John's disciples become disciples of the Nazarene. The crowds that once followed John now gather to follow Jesus. John, however, is pleased with this turn of events, insisting that "He must become greater; I must become less."

John's Persecution
(Mark 6:17-28)

*D*emonstrating his characteristic courage, John tells King Herod that the king's marriage to his sister-in-law Herodias is "unlawful." For delivering that message from God, John is bound and led away to prison while an enraged Herodias seeks for a way to have him executed.

Locked away in his prison cell, John hears news of Jesus' public ministry. He is troubled by doubts about Jesus and sends representatives to ask if Jesus is indeed "the One who was to come." Jesus answers John's questions, then publicly praises him as the greatest man ever born.

The end of John's life comes quickly. During a royal dinner party, King Herod makes a drunken oath to his stepdaughter who, on the advice of her mother, requests the head of John the Baptist. Although Herod is grieved by the request, he yields to the pressure of the moment and has John beheaded.

John's Presentation (Luke 3:1-22)				John's Persecution (Mark 6:17-28)			
John emerges from the desert (Luke 3:1-17)	John baptizes Jesus (Luke 3:21,22)	John identifies Jesus as Messiah (John 1:29-36)	John's public ministry wanes (John 3:26-30)	John's ministry to Herod (Mark 6:17-20)	John's imprisonment by Herod (Mark 6:17)	John's doubts in prison (Matthew 11:2-6)	John's execution by Herod (Matthew 14:3-12)
Jesus, the Nazarene				John, the Martyr			
Announcing King Jesus				Denouncing King Herod			
"I must become less important"				(John 3:30, NIV).			
In the Jordan Valley				In the King's Dungeon			
A.D. 28–31 (33–36 yrs.)				A.D. 28–31 (33–36 yrs.)			

Voice in the Desert

(Read: Matthew 3)

Visualize the prophet Isaiah as he peers into the mists and mysteries of the distant future. Suddenly, he cocks his head to one side, as though hearing some far-away sound . . . like "a voice of one calling (Isa. 40:3a)." What is the message of that distant yet distinct voice?

"In the desert prepare
the way for the Lord;
make straight in the wilderness
a highway for our God. . . .
And the glory of the Lord will be revealed,
and all mankind together will see it.
For the mouth of the Lord has spoken" (Isaiah 40:3,5)

Years pass. Decades. Centuries. The voice of prophecy fades from the land of Israel. But before it does, the nation hears one last prophetic cry, this time from the lips of *Malachi*—"the Lord's messenger." Again, poignant words of prophecy echo in the streets and courtyards of Jerusalem. Solemn words of warning. And yet, words containing a hint of hope.

"See, I will send my messenger, who will prepare the
way before me. Then suddenly the Lord you are seeking
will come . . . . I will send you the prophet Elijah before
that great and dreadful day of the Lord comes."
(Mal. 3:1; 4:5).

The shroud of prophetic silence would cloak Israel for nearly half a millenium, but the nation had something to wait for, something to watch for. Clues. The Lord would come back to judge the nations and bless His people. But before that great and glorious return, there would be a sign: "A voice of one calling in the desert" . . . the appearance of Elijah, the King's herald . . . one who would prepare the way for Israel's long-awaited Messiah.

What then, was the Israelite of A.D. 28 to think when a man clothed in the garments of Elijah emerged from the deserts of Judea? What could this man's cryptic message possibly mean? *"Repent, for the kingdom of heaven is near"* (Matt. 3:1).

The Pharisees and teachers of the Law (who rarely missed an opportunity to display their knowledge of the Scriptures) were determined to discover the "mystery man's" identity.

His words were harsh, almost frightening. They had about them the stern ring of authority, like the prophets of old who had cried up and down the land of Israel. Here was a man who seemed to fear no one—not the religious leaders, not Herod, not even Rome. There was power in the words of this desert man—compelling, authoritative power. Why, he even dared to call the Pharisees and Sadducees a "brood of vipers"! Certainly here was a man to be reckoned with . . . a man to hear . . . perhaps even a man to follow. Rumor had it he might even be the Christ of God (Luke 3:15).

For those who did decide to follow John, there was a curious feeling of unfulfillment. It was as if John had roused a feeling of excitement and attention only to point the seeker in another direction. Everything John said seemed to draw attention away from himself. True, he baptized many and people thronged to the Jordan to hear him preach. But John constantly sought to downplay his popularity.

"I baptize you with water for repentance," John would say. "But after me will come one who is more powerful than I, whose sandals I am not fit to carry. He will baptize you with the Holy Spirit and with fire" (Matt. 3:11).

Nevertheless, rumors about the Baptizer persisted, prompting the priests and Levites to seek him out and discover who he really was. Faced with their queries, he freely confessed, "I am not the Christ."

"They asked him, 'Then who are you? Are you Elijah?'

"He said, 'I am not.'

" 'Are you the Prophet?'

"He answered, 'No.'

"Finally they said, 'Who are you? Give us an answer. What do you say about yourself?'

"John replied in the words of Isaiah the prophet, 'I am the voice of one calling in the desert, *Make straight the way for the Lord* ' " (John 1:20-23, italics added).

One day, as John was baptizing at the Jordan River, a certain man stepped into the current and waded out to meet him. John knew instantly that something was different about this Man. Deep in John's spirit something cried, "Yes! At *last!*" But why did this

One come with the rest—into the waters of repentance? It could not be. Filled with awe and perplexity, John tried to turn Him away.

"I need to be baptized by you," he told the Man. "And do you come to me?" (Matt. 3:13).

But the Man insisted, so John obediently baptized Him. Then, as He came up out of the water, there was a sudden tearing in the fabric of heaven (Mark 1:10). Before John's wondering eyes, the Spirit of God descended in the form of a dove and rested upon the Man he had just baptized. And an audible voice said, "You are my Son, whom I love; with you I am well pleased" (Mark 1:10,11).

From that moment on, John pointed away from himself with even greater urgency.

"He who comes after me has surpassed me" (John 1:15).

"This is the one I meant . . . " (John 1:30).

"I have seen and I testify that this is the Son of God" (John 1:34).

"Look, the Lamb of God who takes away the sin of the world!" (John 1:29).

Two of John's disciples left the Baptizer's side to follow the Man, Jesus. The crowds that had formerly come to John began to diminish. Instead of seeking out the man from the desert, they were now turning to the Man from Galilee. Several of those who still followed John were stung by this apparent rejection of their leader.

John, however, could not have been happier. "The bride belongs to the bridegroom," he explained to his dejected followers. "The friend who attends the bridegroom waits and listens for him, and is full of joy when he hears the bridegroom's voice. That joy is mine, and it is now complete. *He must become greater; I must become less*" (John 3:29,30).

John was a fulfilled man. People were walking right past him on their way to find Jesus. Those who had once attached themselves to the Baptizer were now yearning for a glimpse of the Nazarene, and John said, "My joy is complete! This is the best thing that could have happened to me."

John's whole purpose in life was to introduce others to Jesus

Christ. He was simply a living signpost pointing the way to the Messiah. John's mission would have been a total failure if people had merely stood admiring the directional sign, but going no further. No, everything about John's life said, "On to Jesus! Look to Him."

How can you do the same thing, as one who gladly bears His name? How can your life be a signpost, so that when people see you—when people get to know you—they will be drawn to Jesus?

Think back over the people who have had the greatest influence on your life for Jesus Christ. Try to remember what it was about them that made such a lasting impression on you. Was it their polished testimonies? Their skill in public speaking? Their fame and notoriety?

As I think back, I see the faces of individuals who were anything but public speakers. As a matter of fact, there was little that was smooth or polished about them. I can't remember any of them ever publishing an article or being written up in the newspaper. But there are things I do remember. I remember the meek, plain-looking man who shuffled up to me after church one day and said, "Listen . . . I know . . . uh . . . that it isn't easy being a college student. I know you must have some struggles. I just want you to know my wife and kids and I pray for you every single night."

I hardly knew the man! I was floored. I was humbled. I was deeply touched. But more than that, I saw the love of Jesus in a new way that Sunday.

I remember a roommate in Bible school who experienced a crushing disappointment. I saw him hit bottom. I saw him struggle to rediscover God's perspective. I saw him come through the whole ordeal with a transparent, loving spirit and a trust in Christ that shone like a diamond. But I saw more than that. Through his willingness to be open and unguarded, I saw the grace of Jesus Christ working in his life. It was a glimpse I'll never forget.

There have been other occasions. Kind hands that gripped my shoulder when I felt myself slipping into despair. Eyes that said, "I care, I really do," when I didn't think anyone really did. Voices that spoke gentle, understanding words of counsel when I had no idea which direction to turn.

It hasn't been so much the Christian "superstars" who have touched my life. Oh, on occasion a TV personality or a writer of a book or a singer of a song has compelled me to gaze at Jesus Christ. But more often than not, it's been the people who have taken time to care. It's been the people who have taken the risk to give of themselves. It's been the people who have been honest and transparent enough to show me that Jesus can bring sanity and peace into chaos and pain.

Like John the Baptist, their lives have said to me, "Behold the Lamb of God."

It isn't easy to reach outside of yourself and love someone in the name and power of Jesus. As a matter of fact, it's *risky*. You could be ignored, you could be rejected, you could be rebuffed. Just like Jesus. But then again, you just might break into someone's long night with a shaft of daylight and hope. Because you were willing to take the risk, someone's life may never be the same. But don't be surprised if they look right past you to Jesus Christ.

That's what it's all about.

Doubts in the Dungeon

(Read: Matthew 11)

John the Baptist was no stranger to silence.

How could a man live so many years in the lonely desert without gaining an appreciation—indeed, a *preference*—for long periods of silence?

But the fortress of Machaerus, in Perea, was not the desert. Deep in the damp inner dungeons, there was no sunrise or sunset. There was no caress of wind, no star-filled nights, no tang of wild honey on the tongue. Only a heavy, perpetual night, and silent stone walls.

Perhaps John's brief ministry seemed like a dream to him as he looked back. The crowds . . . the confrontations . . . the lines of eager seekers waiting to be baptized in the clear waters of the Jordan. Had it really happened?

And then there was that moment when he first saw the King. How would John doubt that awe-filled instant when the heavens parted and the dove fluttered down to alight on His shoulder? The

Voice had spoken so clearly—could he ever fail to hear its echo in his heart? *"This is My Son, whom I love; with Him I am well pleased"* (Matt. 3:17).

Everything was as it should be. John had done his job. The crowds were following Jesus. The heart of John, son of Zechariah, should have been enjoying the satisfaction of a task completed. And yet . . .

Why did he feel that piercing needle of doubt?

The road from the Jordan Valley to Herod's prison must have seemed exceedingly short as John pondered his fate day after day.

Would he have done things differently, if he had it all to do over again? Would he have altered his message . . . toned down his harsh condemnation of sin . . . been more "selective" in the targets of his verbal barbs?

Part of John's mission was to reveal and decry sin wherever he found it. So when he saw the self-serving hypocrisy of the religious leaders, he didn't mince words. He told them exactly what they were and how they appeared in the eyes of the God they pretended to serve (Matt. 3:7-10).

And when King Herod divorced his own wife and married Herodias, the wife of his own brother, John confronted him and told him exactly how God felt about it (Matt. 14:3-5).

This was something new. Herod wasn't accustomed to being told how God evaluated his actions. Actually, he wasn't used to anyone evaluating his actions—let alone God.

But John had looked him right in the eye and said, "It is not lawful for you to have your brother's wife" (Mark 6:18). Indeed? The king was stunned. Flabbergasted. But as he listened to this wild-looking preacher, he experienced a storm of mixed emotions. Scripture says that "Herodias nursed a grudge against John and wanted to kill him. But she was not able to, because Herod feared John and protected him, knowing him to be a righteous and holy man. When Herod heard John, he was greatly puzzled, yet he liked to listen to him" (Mark 6:19,20).

Herod kept the Baptizer in "protective custody." He could not release him because of possible political (not to mention domestic) repercussions. Nor could he kill John outright, because the people considered him to be a prophet (Matt. 14:5). And besides, there was something unusual about the man . . . something Herod couldn't quite put his finger on. So he kept John as a prisoner. Day after day. Week after week.

Apparently Herod permitted John to have visitors, for Scripture indicates that John's disciples were allowed to see their leader and bring him information (Matt. 11:2). It was on one of these visits that John finally gave expression to the doubts that had been haunting him in the dungeon.

The messages John had been receiving about the One he had announced were extremely troubling. John knew that Messiah would one day judge the rampant evil in his nation; He would come with an ax in hand to chop down the fruitless trees; He would winnow out the chaff and throw it into the fire while He gathered His wheat into His barn (Matt. 3:11,12). He would come with incredible power and introduce the kingdom of heaven (Matt. 3:2).

But this Man named Jesus of Nazareth seemed to be doing none of these things. The reports being brought by John's disciples were perplexing. Jesus had selected a handful of men to train. He was performing a variety of miracles—gentle, loving acts of mercy. So far He had uttered no words of judgment—no woes upon the nation. Seemingly, His was a mission of mercy, not of judgment.

What was John to think? Had he been mistaken? In his solitude and confusion he cried out for an answer. And so we read, "When John heard in prison what Christ was doing, he sent his disciples to ask him, 'Are you the one who was to come, or should we expect someone else?' " (Matt. 11:2,3).

John's men caught up with Jesus as He was preaching in the towns of Galilee. Hearing his servant's question, He gave this reply:

"Go back and report to John what you hear and see: The blind receive sight, the lame walk, those who have leprosy are cured, the deaf hear, the dead are raised, and the good news is preached to the poor. Blessed is the man who does not fall away on account of me" (Matt. 11:4-6).

At first glance, Jesus' "answer" doesn't seem like an answer at all. What did He mean? Was He simply itemizing His recent miracles so that John—back in prison—would be impressed?

A closer look reveals differently. Jesus was showing John how His ministry *was* fulfilling Old Testament prophecy—specifically Isaiah 35:5,6 and 61:1. He was the expected King—John could rest assured of that. But there were things John did not as yet understand. Christ was going to come *twice*. The first time as Savior, the second time as Judge. The first time as the Lamb of God, the second time as the King of kings. The first time to call sinful men to Himself, the second time to call sinful men to account.

John, like perhaps many an Old Testament prophet, didn't grasp the fact that Jesus had to come twice. Instead, he expected it all to happen at once. When it didn't, he was troubled. He had doubts.

The Lord's reply to His troubled servant was gentle. He didn't berate John for expressing doubts. As a matter of fact, Jesus went on to give him high commendation: "I tell you the truth," He told the crowds, "Among those born of women there has not risen anyone greater than John the Baptist" (Matt 11:11). Nevertheless, in answer to John's doubts, Jesus sent this final reply:

"Happy is the man who never loses faith in Me" (Matt. 11:6, Phillips).

In effect, the Lord was saying, "John, you may not understand My methods or My timing right now. The way I'm going about My work may not be meeting all your expectations. I understand that. But John—can you trust Me? Can you cling to Me, even when you can't understand My ways?"

What was true in John's day is equally true in yours. You can't always see the whole picture. You can't always understand the full scope of God's plans. From your limited human perspective, you may see only a small part of that plan, and perhaps what you see doesn't make much sense to you. You may be troubled and perplexed because God isn't meeting your expectations. Perhaps you feel alone in a difficult situation and God seems indifferent to your prayers.

The question you must face is the same question John faced as he stared at his dungeon walls. The Lord says to you, just as He said to John, "Can you trust My plan even though you cannot *trace* it? Can you put your faith and hope in Me even though you cannot understand My methods or My timing? Can you believe Me that much?"

Perhaps the apostle Paul said it best:

"At present we are men looking at puzzling reflections in a mirror. The time will come when we shall see reality whole and face to face! At present all I know is a little fraction of the truth, but the time will come when I shall know it as fully as God has known me!" (1 Cor. 13:12, Phillips).

Work It Through

1. From an historical perspective, what did John mean when he said of Jesus, "He must become greater; I must become less"? (John 3:30). Can you think of two practical ways this verse can become real in your Christian experience today?

_____

_____

_____

2. Review Mark 6:19,20 and describe Herod's reaction to John's ministry. Why didn't the king have John put to death immediately? Why did he like to listen to this man even though the experience left him both fearful and "greatly puzzled"? What does this tell you about the way your walk affects your talk in the estimation of others?

_____

_____

_____

3. John had certain expectations about Jesus . . . some of which were unfulfilled (Matt. 11:2–6). Name two incorrect expectations that are commonly expressed about God today. Name two other expectations you can safely cling to concerning God and your relationship with Him. (Hint: base them on His clear promises.)

_____

_____

_____

4. According to Matthew 3:8,9, what was the essence of John's warning to the Jews of his day? How could this same warning have a present-day application to the Christians and churches in America?

_____

_____

_____

NOTES

NOTES

Mary of Bethany

Don't fear to call her a disciple because she was a woman. Luke had no such hesitation when referring to another woman, the gentle, generous Tabitha (Acts 9:36). Mary of Bethany was a disciple of Jesus Christ in the truest sense of the word, for she learned His ways and clung to His teaching.

Don't lump her together with her sister Martha either, as though "Mary-and-Martha" were a single homogenous personality rather than two unique and distinct human beings. You would not want to be so treated as indistinguishable from your brother or sister.

And most importantly, don't overlook the transforming message of her life simply because she performed no miracles and did not belong to the company of the Twelve. There is more Scripture devoted to Mary of Bethany then to ten of the twelve male disciples of Jesus Christ. Of what other disciple did Jesus say that his or her name would be held in memory wherever the gospel was preached in the whole world (Matt. 26:13)?

It would be no exaggeration to call Mary of Bethany one of the most significant persons in all of New Testament Scripture. And God put her life in the spotlight for a reason. He wants her life to touch your life, because when it does, you will be changed. For the better.

Mary of Bethany's LIFE IN SUMMARY

Listening at Jesus' Feet (Luke 10:38-42)

*N*ow as they were traveling along, He entered a certain village; and a woman named Martha welcomed Him into her home. And she had a sister called Mary, who moreover was listening to the Lord's word, seated at His feet. But Martha was distracted with all her preparations, and she came up to Him, and said, 'Lord, do you not care that my sister has left me to do all the serving alone? Then tell her to help me.'

"But the Lord answered and said to her, 'Martha, Martha, you are worried and bothered about so many things; but only a few things are necessary, really only one, for Mary has chosen the good part, which shall not be taken away from her' " (Luke 10:38-42 NASB).

Focus	Listening at Jesus' Feet (Luke 10:38–42)
Divisions	Rebuked by Martha: commended by Christ
Topics	The Better Part
	Mary's Priority
	"I Must Hear Him."
Place	Home of Mary (Bethany)
Dates	Approx. Autumn, A.D. 32

Grieving at Jesus' Feet
(John 11:1-46)

*M*artha went away, and called Mary her sister, saying secretly, 'The Teacher is here, and is calling for you.' And when she heard it, she arose quickly, and was coming to Him.

"Now Jesus had not yet come into the village, but was still in the place where Martha met Him. The Jews then who were with her in the house, and consoling her, when they saw that Mary rose up quickly and went out, followed her, supposing that she was going to the tomb to weep there. Therefore, when Mary came where Jesus was, she saw Him, and fell at His feet, saying to Him, 'Lord if You had been here, my brother would not have died.' When Jesus therefore saw her weeping . . . He was deeply moved in spirit, and was troubled, and said, 'Where have you laid him?' They said to Him, 'Lord, come and see.' Jesus wept." (John 11:28-35 NASB).

Ministering at Jesus' Feet
(Mark 14:3-6,8,9)

*W*hile he was in Bethany, reclining at the table in the home of a man known as Simon the Leper, a woman came with an alabaster jar of very expensive perfume, made of pure nard. She broke the jar and poured the perfume on his head.

"Some of those present were saying indignantly to one another, 'Why this waste of perfume? It could have been sold for more than a year's wages and the money given to the poor.' And they rebuked her harshly.

" 'Leave her alone,' said Jesus. 'Why are you bothering her? She has done a beautiful thing to me . . . She did what she could. She poured perfume on my body beforehand to prepare for my burial. I tell you the truth, wherever the gospel is preached throughout the world, what she has done will also be told, in memory of her' " (Mark 14:3-6,8,9 NIV).

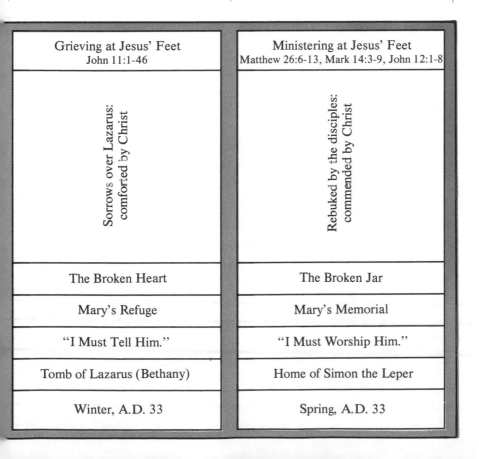

Grieving at Jesus' Feet John 11:1-46	Ministering at Jesus' Feet Matthew 26:6-13, Mark 14:3-9, John 12:1-8
Sorrows over Lazarus: comforted by Christ	Rebuked by the disciples: commended by Christ
The Broken Heart	The Broken Jar
Mary's Refuge	Mary's Memorial
"I Must Tell Him."	"I Must Worship Him."
Tomb of Lazarus (Bethany)	Home of Simon the Leper
Winter, A.D. 33	Spring, A.D. 33

The Better Choice

(Read: Luke 10:38-42)

The early rains had already begun, softening the sun-baked soil and reminding farmers that it was time to sharpen their plows. With the freshening wind and welcome rain the Teacher followed the well-rutted path from the north as He approached Jersualem.

Back in the rolling foothills of Galilee, where He and His men had been staying for a number of months, Jesus had told a roadside inquirer, "Foxes have holes and birds of the air have nests, but the Son of Man has no place to lay His head" (Luke 9:58). Nevertheless, as He drew near to the ancient city of Jerusalem, Jesus knew where He would lay his head. It was not to be His own home, nor the home of a relative. And yet, it was to be a place every bit as welcome to His knock.

Jesus' steps took Him to the abode of two sisters, Martha and Mary, and their brother Lazarus. There in the village of Bethany, close at hand to the city of Jerusalem and to the place where He would soon die, the Teacher knew He would find shelter, refreshment for body and soul, and the love of devoted friends. If He was not *at home* in Bethany, at least He could *feel* at home. And for a few precious hours, the Man of Sorrows could bask in the warmth of caring human companionship.

It was Martha who greeted the small, travel-weary company at the door. The house into which she invited them was "*her* home" (Luke 10:38), indicating perhaps she was older than Mary and Lazarus and carried full responsibility for the household affairs.

We are not told whether Jesus sent advance word to the Bethany home that He was coming. Quite possibly He did. Knowing the privilege that was soon to be hers, Martha apparently threw herself into a frenzy of activity, preparing a large meal and comfortable sleeping quarters for the Master and His men.

As only a homemaker who entertains company on short notice can appreciate, Martha felt under pressure. She knew Who her Guest was to be. She knew what an unspeakable honor was soon to be hers. And Martha loved Jesus. So when He came through that front door, everything had to be perfect. No doubt both she and Mary labored long and hard to make it so. The meal . . . well, it certainly couldn't be *average*. This was no visiting cousin or haughty Pharisee. This was *the Christ*. The very Son of God! What a privilege to serve Him. But—oh! What a responsibility.

So much to do. An extra trip to the market for provisions. Hurried visits to the neighbors to borrow extra utensils and sleeping mats. The house had to be immaculate. Every vase needed flowers. Every lamp needed extra oil. In all these preparations, there is no reason to assume Mary and Martha did not share the toil equally.

When Jesus and His disciples were finally settled within the house, Martha felt no release from the pressure. Rather, it seemed to grow with each passing minute. So much to do . . . and so little time! The dinner preparations must have seemed endless as Martha thought of "added touches" to enhance her culinary masterpiece.

How Martha must have looked forward to this day! And yet, now that it was here, she had so little time to enjoy it. Had she even had time to say more than a quick greeting to the Master? Perhaps not, but then—surely He would understand. Sauces simmering on the fire . . . bread browning in the oven . . . baskets of fruit that needed to be washed and prepared. In spite of her best efforts, the meal was falling farther and farther behind schedule and—*where in the world was Mary?*

Had she callously deserted her sister at the moment Martha needed her most? Had she thoughtlessly left Martha with all the work of preparing the meal?

It would have been easy to draw that conclusion. Here was Martha, red-faced and ruffled, running here and there, perpetually in motion. And there was sister Mary—cool and composed. Every hair in place. Sitting at the Master's feet as if that was the most important thing in the world. Well, Martha wanted to hear the Lord's words, too. But . . . .

One translation says of Martha she was "very worried about her elaborate preparations." The Greek word used by Luke literally means "to be drawn away or distracted." Martha was certainly that! But from whom was she drawn away? From what was she distracted? The answer is revealing. Martha's "much serving" drew her *away from her Lord!* Her "elaborate preparations" were distracting her attention from His words and counsel.

Jesus wasn't standing in the middle of the house shouting at the top of His lungs. Nevertheless, He *was* speaking. Seated on a bench or chair, He was quietly sharing truths to sustain the hearts of His loved ones during the coming days of trial. Mary, seated at His feet, hung on His every word, absorbed His every phrase, cherished every inflection of His voice.

Back in the kitchen, Martha was missing out. She was making too much noise to hear His voice. She was too occupied with watching the bread and dicing the figs to respond to His counsel. Was it fair? Why didn't the Lord raise His voice so that she could hear, too? Why didn't He get up from His chair and speak in the kitchen while she "peeled the potatoes and polished the silver"? Why didn't He just make small talk until she could finish up her tasks and join them in the living room?

Martha had a lot to learn about the way the Lord works. He doesn't shout. He doesn't use a megaphone. Nevertheless, He *does* speak. Continually. Quietly. To those who are listening for the sound of His voice. And if a believer wants to grow closer to Him, there comes a time when he or she must put aside *activity* and take a seat *attentively* at the Master's feet.

Isn't that what Martha wanted? A closer relationship with Jesus Christ? Because of her love for the Lord, she leaped at the opportunity to serve Him. Nothing was too good for the Master. No sacrifice of time, resource, or energy was too great.

And yet, for all her zeal and perspiration, the net result of Martha's service was to *draw her away from Christ.* This was evident when she burst into the room, lashed out at her sister, and criticized the Lord for not taking Mary to task.

At that point the Lord (who knew Martha much better than Martha knew herself) gently put His finger on the major spiritual problem in her life.

"Martha, Martha," He said, "you are worried and bothered about so many things; but only a few things are necessary, really only one" (Luke 10:41,42 NASB)

On one level Jesus may have been saying, "Martha, my harried hostess, all of these elaborate preparations and fancy dishes really aren't necessary. Something simple would have been just fine."

On a deeper level, however, Jesus' words may have carried

another message. "Martha, you know that I appreciate your sincere service—and I know you mean to honor Me by working so hard and doing the best you can. But Martha . . . you've allowed your work *for* Me to distract from your time *with* Me. And I would rather have your companionship, My daughter, than your service. I would rather that you hear My words and understand My counsel than go the extra mile in much serving."

It isn't a matter of either/or. It isn't that Mary was spiritual because she sat quietly and Martha was carnal because she served vigorously. Both sisters must have toiled diligently to get ready for their guest. Jesus would not have commended Mary if she had avoided her responsibilities and saddled her sister with all the work. Undoubtedly, Mary served as wholeheartedly as Martha. But there was a difference. Mary knew where to draw the line. Mary realized that when Jesus was speaking, her number one priority in life was listening. She knew that, important as it was to serve Him at the table, it is even more important to worship at His feet.

"Mary has chosen what is better," Jesus told Martha, "and it will not be taken away from her" (Luke 10:42).

It is possible for you to choose the good and yet miss the best. Being involved in the Lord's work—church activities, Sunday school, seminars, home Bible studies—is good. As a matter of fact, it is *very* good. Paul affirmed this in 1 Corinthians 15:58 when he said, "Always give yourselves fully to the work of the Lord, because you know that your labor in the Lord is not in vain."

What a comfort to realize that all your toil and effort in the Savior's name will bear eternal results. God is acutely aware of all that you do for His sake (cf. Rev. 2:2).

Nevertheless, the Enemy would be delighted to see a believer so preoccupied with "doing" that he or she no longer has time for "being" alone with God. Satan scores a major victory whenever a Christian's schedule becomes so overloaded with "good" activities that quiet, reflective moments in God's Word and in prayer are squeezed out of the day.

Perhaps there have been times in your life this week when the Lord has wanted to say to you, "My dear child, you are worried and bothered or distracted by so many *things*. But you have no time for Me! You have no time to sit at My feet and hear My voice. Why not set aside "serving" for awhile and allow Me to serve you? Come apart with Me and rest awhile. Refresh yourself in My presence. Listen to My words of guidance and counsel. And by the way . . . I love you. I would rather have your fellowship than your service. Choose the better part. It will never be taken away from you."

"She Did What She Could . . . "

(Read: John 12:1-9)

It should have been a happy occasion.

All the ingredients were present for a warm, pleasant evening of conversation and companionship. Jesus and His disciples were back in Bethany. They were all gathered around a supper table at the home of a friend known as Simon the Leper (the "leper" part no doubt a lingering reminder of days gone by before the Great Physician came to town). Martha was serving again, so the food was undoubtedly superb. Gentle Mary was there, of course, as close to the Teacher as she could get. And Lazarus. *Lazarus!* Alive from the dead!

It was an awesome thing to look across the table at Lazarus, eating with good appetite, his eyes clear and sparkling, his voice hearty and strong. Could it be? Could this really be the same man who had grown so ill and feeble? Could this be the same man whose breathing grew shallow, who finally gave a little sigh and passed into eternity? Was this indeed the Lazarus whose cold, rigid body the two grieving sisters had tenderly washed, wrapped in cloth and spices, and sealed in a dark tomb?

It was he. Among them once again. A living testimony to the limitless power and compassion of the one who called Himself the Resurrection and the Life.

It should have been a joyful dinner party. Full of laughter and praise. Gladness and singing.

But it wasn't.

Instead, the atmosphere was heavy with tension—charged with impending crisis and nameless dread. There were haunting recollections of the Teacher's recent words—repeated assertions that He was going to suffer and die. Soon. In shameful humiliation. At the hand of the Gentiles. Word was out in the city and suburbs that the Nazarene was wanted by the authorities. The temple police were on special alert. The religious leaders had emissaries everywhere. Watching. Waiting.

Around the supper table, emotions simmered just below the surface. Smiles were quick and tense. A number of faces looked openly worried or preoccupied. Perhaps tears brimmed in the eyes of some. The joy of having Lazarus back in full health seemed somehow overshadowed, like a bright spring day marred by clouds gathering on the horizon.

No one could think of anything appropriate to say or do. Given such a silent, somber setting, Mary's sudden movement must have startled everyone. Without a word she left the room and then reappeared carrying a jar. A stunningly beautiful jar of white alabaster. It is easy to imagine every eye riveted upon this unpredictable sister of Martha and Lazarus. What was she going to do with that jar? Why was she walking toward the Teacher? Perhaps a collective gasp went up from the group as the woman deliberately broke off the top of the jar and began to pour its contents over the head of Jesus. Before anyone could gather his wits or say anything, she emptied the broken vessel over His feet and tenderly began to wipe His feet with her long, flowing hair. A murmur of anger and disgust went up from the gathering even as the sweet, haunting odor of pure nard swept through the room.

Judas was not the only one to object. Scripture indicates that a number began to complain. " 'Why this waste of perfume?' one of them demanded. 'It could have been sold for more than a year's wages and the money given to the poor' " (Mark 14:4,5).

Think about that statement for a moment before you rush to Mary's defense. Put the "year's wages" on today's scale. If a man or woman today earns a modest salary of $1,000 a month, a year's wages would equal $12,000. Now imagine a $12,000 item being poured out . . . expended . . . ruined in a single moment. Mary shattered the jar and poured out the precious liquid in a seemingly impetuous, careless action.

Perhaps the perfume had been Mary's carefully treasured dowry, saved over the years in anticipation of a future wedding day. Perhaps the nard had long remained hidden away in a personal hope chest. Undoubtedly, the liquid represented a major portion of Mary's inheritance—perhaps a life's savings.

No one else could have known what that alabaster jar meant to Mary. Certainly not the disciples. Perhaps not even Martha or Lazarus.

But Jesus knew. Looking into Mary's eyes, He knew exactly what hopes, longings, and dreams were bound up in that pint of perfume. He knew what it meant for Mary to shatter that jar and pour it over His feet. He understood. *And it moved Jesus Christ to the depth of His being. It touched the very heart of God.*

With a wave of His hand He silenced the shallow mutterings of those who saw only the external and monetary loss. He dismissed their callous criticism and rebuked their warped, insensitive hearts.

"Why do you bother her—why do you trouble this woman's heart and spoil this priceless moment? Mary has done a beautiful thing to Me."

In Mark 14:8 Jesus said, *"She did what she could."* She gave what she had. She poured out her most precious possession in utter abandonment.

More than anyone else in the room—perhaps more than anyone else in the world—Mary of Bethany identified with the Lord's approaching horror. As the dark hour of Calvary approached, gripping His soul with its black promise of agony and utter aloneness, it was a *woman* who reached out to the Son of Man. It was a *woman* who sensed His need and moved to His side to support Him.

She did what she could. The best she knew how. Careless of self. Heedless of criticism. Filled only with love for Him. And the Man of Sorrows saw a small ray of light in the gathering gloom. For a brief moment, His troubled heart was warmed by a spontaneous expression of love.

How seldom in the gospels do you encounter an individual who actually ministered to the Lord Jesus. Typically, it was Jesus who healed, Jesus who comforted, Jesus who fed the hungry, Jesus who gave of Himself freely, ultimately giving His very life.

But Mary was one of the very few who gave something back to

Him—who reached out in a tangible way and brought warmth and blessing to the heart of the Savior. "She did what she could."

What can *you* do? How can you, as a believer today, bless the heart of God? What cherished "alabaster jar" can you bring to pour out before Him?

Your *praise* ministers to Him. Hebrews 13:15 says, "Let us, then, always offer praise to God as our sacrifice through Jesus, which is the offering presented by lips that confess His name" (GNB). When, in your prayers, you set aside time to simply pour out your heart in praise and thanksgiving, that is pleasing to the Lord. Similarly, when you speak well of Him before others, declaring who He is and what He has done, you are bringing glory to His name. You are ministering to God.

Most of all, however, God simply wants you. Paul says it best in Romans 12:1,2—"I urge you, brothers, in view of God's mercy, to offer your bodies as living sacrifices, holy and *pleasing to God*—which is your spiritual worship. Do not conform any longer to the pattern of this world, but be transformed by the renewing of your mind. Then you will be able to test and approve what God's will is—his good, pleasing and perfect will" (italics added).

It isn't easy to put yourself on the altar. It could mean some broken pride, broken ambitions, broken plans, broken dreams. Life is precious—it's painfully hard to let go. Mary's jar looked so beautiful tucked away in her hope chest. But when she broke it, pouring it all out at the Master's feet, the fragrance wafted far beyond that tiny room in Bethany. Jesus saw to it that it filled the whole world. Two thousand years later, its fragrance lingers on.

Jesus has a way of doing that with broken jars.

Work It Through

1. Martha apparently worked very hard to prepare an elaborate meal for Jesus and His disciples. Was Jesus implying to her that it was unwise to "go the extra mile" in exercising hospitality? Explain your answer.

_____

_____

2. What was Jesus referring to in Luke 10:41 when He told Martha that only "one thing" was necessary or needful?

_____

_____

3. Luke 10:38-41 seems to suggest that work _for_ Christ is no substitute for time _with_ Christ. How can a believer make sure that he or she has the right balance between the two? Evaluate the balance in your own Christian life.

_____

_____

4. How did some of the disciples "miss the mark" when they harshly criticized Mary for pouring out her valuable perfume on the Lord? What illustrations of this mistaken perspective can you cite in the work of the Lord today in your own local church? In your own personal or professional life?

_____

_____

5. What are some 20th-century "broken jars" that come to mind as fitting expressions of _your_ love and devotion for God?

_____

_____

NOTES

Timothy

Imagine a historian, centuries in the future, trying to piece together the details of *your life*. Suppose that scholar came across several lengthy letters addressed to you from one of your closest friends. What might the historian discover about *you*—your personality, your strengths, your weaknesses—from simply examining the letters of your friend?

Those who have studied the life of Timothy have had little to go on other than the two letters addressed to him by the apostle Paul. As a matter of fact, you have access to those same two letters, the ones we know as First and Second Timothy. Nineteen centuries have passed since those epistles were penned and posted. But an incredible thing happens when, with the guidance of God's Spirit, those personal notes are carefully examined. Timothy becomes more than a"Bible name," more than a stained-glass saint. He begins to emerge as a warm, flesh-and-blood human being. A young man who struggled with issues like finances, personal purity, commitment to his job and the give-and-take of interpersonal relationships. A person who felt the crunch of pressure, the gnaw of anxiety, the sting of rejection, the pang of loneliness, as well as the cold stab of fear. Paul's counsel to his young understudy includes an insightful look at the meaning of *contentment*. From Timothy's point of view that advice couldn't have been more timely. Perhaps it will prove timely for you as well.

Timothy, the Devout Youth

Born and raised in the Asian city of Lystra (now a part of modern Turkey), Timothy may have witnessed the dramatic ministry and miracles of Paul and Barnabas as the two missionaries passed through Asia on their first missionary journey. Assuming that to be true, the young man may have also viewed the ensuing riot where Paul was stoned by the angry crowd, left for dead, then revived to life.

The son of a Greek father and a Jewish mother (Eunice), Timothy grows up in a household where the Scriptures are held in high esteem. Both Timothy and his mother may have come to faith in Christ during Paul's first visit to their city. As he matures, Timothy grows strong in the Lord, studying the Scriptures and encouraging the believers in Lystra and nearby Iconium.

Focus	Timothy, the Devout Youth				
Divisions	Born of mixed parentage (Acts 16:3)	Learns holy Scriptures as a child (2 Tim 3:15)	Grows up in Lystra (Acts 16:1)	Becomes a Christian under Paul's ministry (Acts 14:8-23; 1 Tim. 1:2)	Enjoys favor of believers in Lystra and Iconium (Acts 16:2)
Topics	Building the foundation				
	Taught by Lois and Eunice				
	Student of the Word				
Place	Lystra				
Approx. Dates (Age)	A.D. 33–53 (Birth–20 yrs.)				

Timothy, the Devoted Apprentice

Because of his reputation as a whole-hearted young disciple of Jesus Christ, Timothy is asked to accompany Paul on his second missionary journey. In order to remove any possible hindrances to Timothy's usefulness in the work of evangelization among the Jews, Paul circumcises his young associate.

For nearly a decade, Timothy ministers at Paul's side or in Paul's behalf in cities and towns around the Roman world. He becomes one of Paul's most trusted lieutenants, sharing the apostle's dangers, triumphs, disappointments and affections for the struggling new churches. Timothy accompanies Paul on the apostle's final trip to Jerusalem. When Paul is imprisoned in Rome, Timothy remains loyally at his side.

Timothy, the Dependable Leader

While with the imprisoned Paul, Timothy co-authors the books of Philippians, Colossians and Philemon. Upon Paul's release from Roman custody, Timothy is dispatched to Philippi, bearing news of the release. He later meets Paul in Ephesus, where the apostle encounters heretical teachers. As Paul prepares for a tour of Macedonia, he instructs Timothy to remain in Ephesus in order to counter the persistent problem of false teachers.

Timid and sickly by nature, Timothy struggles with the Ephesian assignment. Writing from Macedonia, Paul encourages his companion with words of counsel and challenge. Several years later, Timothy (apparently still in Ephesus) receives another letter from Paul informing him that the apostle is near death in a Roman prison. Paul urges Timothy to join him there before it is too late.

Timothy, the Devoted Apprentice				Timothy, the Dependable Leader			
Joins Paul on 2nd missionary journey (Acts 16:3-5)	Serves as Paul's messenger (1 Thess. 3:1,2; Acts 18:5; Rom. 16:21)	Ministers at Paul's side (1 Thess. 3:1,2; Acts 18:5; Rom. 16:21)	Accompanies Paul to Rome; shares prison experience (Acts. 20:4; Phil. 2:14-20)	Pastors in Ephesus (1 Tim., 2 Tim.)	Urged by Paul to join him in Rome (2 Tim. 4:9-13)	Released from imprisonment (Heb. 13:23)	Continuing Christian service (Heb. 13:23)
Practicing the principles				Meeting the challenge			
Taught by Paul				Taught by Paul			
Understudy of the Apostle				Steward of the ministry			
On the road with Paul				Ephesus			
A.D. 53–62 (20–29 yrs.)				A.D. 63–? (30 yrs.–Death)			

Be Content With What You Have

(Read: 1 Timothy 1-6)

Hearing the words "the early church," you perhaps envision a golden era of delightful unity, fervent faith, and boundless zeal. The stirring words of Luke come quickly to mind: "All of the believers were one in heart and mind. No one claimed that any of his possessions was his own, but they shared everything they had" (Acts 4:32).

It is easy to forget that only a few decades later "the early church" was fighting for its very life. On one side was the malicious jealousy of frustrated Judaism; on the other, the strangling influence of decadent paganism. And over it all the iron heel of Rome.

The A.D. 60's were not an easy time to pastor a church. Particularly a troubled, struggling church. Particularly if you were a timid, introspective individual who tended toward stomach trouble (2 Tim. 1:7; 1 Tim. 5:23). And yet that is precisely where Timothy found himself. Given the difficult situation in Ephesus, Timothy perhaps yearned to take an immediate "leave of absence" and rejoin his beloved mentor, the apostle Paul, out on the missionary circuit. How different even hopeless situations must have looked with the irrepressible man from Tarsus by your side!

From all indications, the letter we know as First Timothy was written after the apostle had been released from his first Roman imprisonment but before his second and final confinement. The letter was probably penned while the aging missionary was revisiting some of the churches he had founded in the province of Macedonia. Paul's confinement had been long, and no doubt he was now trying to make up for "lost time," sensing that his days of freedom might be limited.

But if Timothy had been hoping against hope for some reprieve from his difficult duties as he opened the letter from his friend, he was in for a disappointment. No sooner had Paul completed his greeting than Timothy's anxious eyes encountered these significant words: "As I urged you when I went into Macedonia, stay there in Ephesus so that you may command certain men not to teach false doctrines any longer . . . " (1 Tim. 1:3).

How those four words must have stung! "Stay there in Ephesus." Stick with it. Don't bail out. Continue the struggle.

Certainly not the words Timothy was looking for . . . longing for. The sentence he really wanted to read would not come until later . . . years later . . . when his beleaguered teacher was in a Roman prison, near death. At that time, Paul wrote:

"Do your best to come to me quickly" (2 Tim. 4:9).

But for now, that was not to be. Paul's letter to his young associate urged him to remain with the Ephesian flock. Rather than an order to "Retreat!," it was filled with counsel on how to face the many delicate problems that this pastorate presented.

One of the problems seemed particularly touchy, and cut cross-grained against the mindset of the Ephesian society. It was an issue that touched every member of the assembly in a highly personal way—the issue of money.

G. Campbell Morgan paints the scene like this:

> We have to remember the condition of Ephesus at this time; it was the center of abounding commerce; its citizens were mastered by a passion for wealth. The supreme ambition in the activities of the city was that of getting gain. There was, moreover, a strange religious aspect of all this . . . . Ephesus was the place where the temple to Diana stood, and that temple had become to the merchant-men of the city both sanctuary and bank; it was the place of their worship, and it was the place where they deposited their gains. The worship of Diana had become in itself the very essence of devotion to the getting of gain. Ephesus was in the grip of the lust for gold.

Somehow, word got back to Paul that the materialistic, money-hungry attitude of Ephesus was worming its way into the doctrines of the church as well. Certain false teachers had arisen in the assembly who were diluting the gospel of Christ with an appeal to men's greed. Becoming a Christian, they maintained, was a sure path to financial prosperity (cf. 1 Tim. 6:5).

If Paul had been personally present, these "prosperity preachers" would have been promptly put in their place. But he was not, and it fell to young Timothy to confront the propagators of this heresy. Paul was angry. As he wrote to advise his lieutenant on how to handle the situation, the apostle's pen flowed with heated ink:

"If anyone teaches false doctrines and does not agree to the sound doctrine of our Lord Jesus Christ and to godly teaching, he is conceited and understands nothing" (1 Tim. 6:3).

The New English Bible gives the last phrase a sharper edge: "He is a pompous ignoramus."

There were serious problems for the church in this strategic Asiatic city. The task of providing spiritual leadership in such an environment was staggering. Paul himself had referred to the "wild beasts in Ephesus" (1 Corinthians 15:32) . . . and he wasn't talking about the local zoo. As he wrote from Macedonia, the apostle had two heavy concerns on his heart: one for the *ministry* in Ephesus and the other for the *minister*.

As for the ministry, Ephesus was a vital city, both culturally and geographically. It was essential to maintain a clear, ringing witness for the risen Lord in that place, even in the face of hostility and opposition. Knowing full well Timothy's limitations, Paul entrusted the Ephesian charge into the young man's hands.

Timothy himself was a deep concern to the apostle. Since that day in Lystra when he joined Paul's missionary team, Timothy had proved himself a valuable asset. Coming so soon after Paul's painful parting with Barnabas, the companionship and fresh enthusiasm of this devout young disciple must have been especially welcome (cf. Acts 15:36-16:5). Timothy accompanied Paul for the remainder of the missionary journey, and some time later, he joined his leader behind the bars of a Roman prison (cf. Phil. 1:1; Col. 1:1). The relationship of Paul to Timothy was more than merely teacher and pupil—it was more akin to that of father and beloved son (cf. 1 Tim. 1:2; 2 Tim. 1:2-4).

So the apostle bore these twin concerns as he traveled: the Ephesians were becoming distracted and discontented with their financial status, and Timothy was becoming increasingly discontented with the Ephesians. A tonic was needed for both of these ailments, and Paul proceeded to write out a prescription.

The "prosperity preachers" in the Ephesian church had selected a motto for themselves, and no doubt enjoyed quoting it to one another at every opportunity:

"GODLINESS MEANS GAIN!" (cf. 1 Tim. 6:5).

This was apparently the message they were bearing to the Ephesian community. Paraphrased, their appeal might sound something like this:

"What are your dreams? Do you want to be rich? Do you long to own a larger villa? Wouldn't you love to get behind the reins of a shiny new chariot? Wouldn't you enjoy the prestige of sending your kids to school in Athens? How would you like to see dramatic financial gains that would astound your friends and confound your foes? Do these things sound good to you? *Then become a Christian!* Get on God's payroll and be a winner all the way around!"

It sounded so appealing. (Particularly in the Ephesian culture.) Perhaps even Timothy was having a difficult time keeping a grip on God's perspective.

In his counsel, Paul conceded that even he had to agree with part of the philosophy. They're right, Timothy. Godliness *does* mean gain— gain beyond imagining. But only when it is coupled with contentment!"

Godliness with contentment is great gain" (1 Tim. 6:6).

Contentment? It wasn't a well-known word in the get-ahead Ephesian business community. Stoic philosophers of the day were greatly fond of the word, and they used it frequently. To them it meant a sense of independence—a cool indifference to the circumstances of life. Paul, however, had something far deeper in mind than stony, Stoic indifference. To Paul, contentment meant a heartfelt *satisfaction* with whatever situation God placed him in.

In his letter to the Philippians, he put it like this:

I have learned to be content whatever the circumstances. I know what it is to be in need, and I know what it is to have plenty. I have learned the secret of being content in any and every situation, whether well-fed or hungry, whether living in plenty or want (Phil. 4:11,12).

Tell the people to find contentment with what God gives them, the apostle urged Timothy. When you can simply rest in Him and in His provision, without becoming anxious or upset, you have found great gain— you have found true prosperity.

201

But what happens to those who get carried away with the desire to become wealthy? Paul's warning was grim. Those who follow that road will fall into a trap and find themselves "pierced with many griefs" (cf. 1 Tim. 6:9). Paul's choice of words calls to mind the description of a crude but deadly-efficient trap that was once used to snare wild beasts. The body of a small animal would be used as bait, suspended over a lightly covered pit to be impaled on sharpened stakes below.

The lust for more and more "things" can be like that, Paul told Timothy. The bait is attractive—very tantalizing—but there are ugly perils hidden just beyond view. Throw yourself into a lifestyle of getting and gathering and your gain may be more than you bargained for: grief... broken health... broken home... broken dreams.

The alternative? Once again, Paul's counsel is both stern and clear: "Command those who are rich in this present world not to be arrogant nor put their hope in wealth, which is so uncertain, but to put their hope in God, who richly provides us with everything for our enjoyment" (1 Tim. 6:17).

"Timothy," Paul was saying, "as shepherd of the flock you have a responsibility to some of those under your charge. You need to sit them down, look them straight in the eye, and tell them they are building their lives on a crumbling foundation. *Command them* to tear their hopes from the good-paying jobs, the fat bank accounts and the high-yield money market certificates. Tell them to pin their hopes and expectations on God alone—the very One who said 'Never will I leave you; never will I forsake you,'" (Heb. 13:5).

Such was Paul's counsel to the Christians living under the shadow of Diana's temple. It was now up to Timothy to deliver the message with all the tools God had provided him: with power, with love, and with self-control beyond his years (cf. 2 Tim. 1:7). The apostle's exhortation, however, was a two-edged sword, piercing the one who wielded it as well as those at whom it was thrust. Timothy also needed to learn something about contentment.

Be Content Where You Are

(Read: 2 Timothy 1-4)

When Paul said, "Godliness with *contentment* is great gain," Timothy was undoubtedly aware that the implications of his friend's words went far beyond finances.

Timothy himself seemed to be locked in a deep struggle with this question of inner contentment. A number of Bible expositors have drawn this assumption from the tone and content of Paul's two letters to his young associate. Passages like 1 Timothy 1:3,18; 4:12, 15,16; 5:21; 6:12,20; 2 Timothy 1:6-9; 2:1-8; 4:1,2 might indicate that Timothy's grip was slipping—that he needed a new infusion of God's grace in order to face his responsibilities in Ephesus.

The apostle's words about contentment could have been paraphrased this way: "Timothy, I know you want to leave that messy situation in Ephesus. I know you don't feel cut out for the job. I know there are those who look down on you because you are young (1 Tim. 4:12). I know your heart is with me—out here on the missionary trail. But Timothy, you're needed in Ephesus right now. God has placed you there under my authority. There's a job to be done and He wants you to do it. Can you be content with that? Can you rest your anxieties and fears in His hands and pour yourself into the tough task at hand?"

It wouldn't be easy. Timothy was a sensitive man, and no doubt shed many tears in private (cf. 2 Tim. 1:4). But he persevered. And later on, he was able to realize the desire of his heart and rejoin his spiritual father once again (2 Tim. 6:19,20).

But wait a minute. Was Paul saying that a believer is never to dream—never to aspire to greater things? Was he saying that you are simply to fold your hands, and not try to better your situation, whatever it may be?

No, not at all. But Paul wanted Timothy to grasp an important and potentially life-changing truth.

Situations change. Circumstances shift. Life is in flux. The financial prosperity that comes like the first ray of sunshine after a summer storm may just as abruptly fade. The good job, the good health, the golden days when everything is going right—can all change. Overnight. In the blink of an eye.

Nevertheless . . . a Christian can be *content*. Satisfied. At peace.

He can know that whatever comes into his life enters only by his loving Father's permission (cf. Job 1:8-12) and will result in his ultimate good (Rom. 8:28).

Some of the Ephesian Christians had become so prosperity-conscious, so tied to their material possessions and comfortable lifestyle that they would not have been able to handle a sudden change. Paul knew if the economy faltered or the government's attitude toward Christians suddenly changed for the worse—these brothers and sisters would lose their spiritual equilibrium. They would simply not be able to meet the test.

By contrast, Paul's *attitude* allowed for *latitude.* He knew, for instance, that as an apostle he would most likely be spending some time in prison. Did he relish that prospect? Did he enjoy the thought of being separated from his friends, locked away in a dark and lonely dungeon? Of course not. And once he was in prison, did he try to obtain release? Absolutely. But what was his state of mind while he waited for news of his efforts? *He was content.* Satisfied. At peace. He could weather the situation because he knew that even as Caesar's prisoner, he was a free man in Jesus Christ. If his money ran out, he had true riches that would never fade (cf. 1 Tim. 6:18,19). If his health faltered, he knew that his inner self was being renewed every day, and that a new body awaited him around the corner (cf. 2 Cor. 4:16; 5:1,2).

Did that mean Paul had lost interest in being free, in having money or in maintaining good health? No! But neither did he pin his hopes on these things. His hope was in God, and he could be content with whatever God brought his way (1 Tim. 6:17).

No believer can live life totally *above* his circumstances. A Christian, however, can live within his circumstances—even while seeking to change them—and enjoy real contentment and peace.

Contentment is so elusive. It is so easy to fall into the trap of resting the full weight of your hopes and expectations on the outcome of certain circumstances. "If only this happens . . . if only he calls . . . if only she writes . . . if only I get that job . . . if only I get that raise . . . if only we could afford that new house . . . if only that transfer comes through . . . ." Life becomes so filled with the "if-onlys" of the future that TODAY becomes an inconvenient obstacle in the path of reaching tomorrow. And yet, today is all you have! Life is filled with todays, and God wants His dearly-loved children to live each one with contentment.

Dear Father,

I realize that Your desire for me is true contentment of heart. Your Word says that godliness with contentment is great gain. I confess, Lord, that this kind of contentment often escapes me. So many of my thoughts are consumed with tomorrow and what might happen, that I have given very little consideration to today—to this new day You have given me in Your grace.

Help me, Lord, to learn the secret that Paul so desperately wanted to pass along to his son in the faith. In the midst of a society wrapped up with money and the getting of "things," help me to focus my thoughts on the true riches which only You can provide. By the power of Your indwelling Spirit, begin to reshape my value system so that it more closely resembles Your own.

Most of all, help me to be a contented man—a contented woman—in whatever situation You choose to bring into my life today. Help me Lord, as only You can, to live THIS DAY to the full. For Jesus' sake, Amen.

Work It Through

1. *Contentment* is sometimes equated with "putting up with the status quo." How was Paul's exhortation to Timothy more than simply a command to "stay put"?

_____

_____

_____

2. *Contentment* often requires postponing personal plans or cherished ambitions. What would Timothy have *liked* to have read in Paul's first letter, and how did his response to Paul's words show the true character of his Christian maturity?

_____

_____

_____

3. The situation facing the church in Ephesus was difficult, and Timothy was a rather dubious candidate (from a human perspective) to pastor the flock of God there. What were Timothy's *liabilities* as he faced the task (i.e., his age, health, etc.) and what were his *assets* (i.e., his godly heritage)?

_____

_____

_____

4. The key to Timothy's success . . . and yours . . . in the particular area of service God has for each of you is found in 1 Timothy 6:6—"Godliness with contentment is great gain." After reading about Timothy's challenging life, can you paraphrase that verse in your own words? What is one specific way you can *practice godliness* and *demonstrate contentment* in your Christian walk today?

_____

_____

_____

NOTES